WHY WE TEACH SCIENCE (AND WHY WE SHOULD)

Science education isn't just for producing future scientists. It's for producing science literate citizens. The benefits of science literacy, long accepted in US education, are now being questioned and even attacked. In *Why We Teach Science*, Rudolph examines how well science education has served this purpose and finds it lacking. He argues for a new approach to teaching science, one that meets the needs of a science literate society.

Gale M. Sinatra, University of Southern California.
Co-Author of *Science Denial: Why It Happens*
And What to Do About It

In *Why We Teach Science and Why We Should*, John Rudolph provocatively interrogates the discrepancy between the professed aims of American science education and the way in which it is actually conducted, ending with a compelling plea to reorient science education to serve science and society effectively.

Glenn Branch, deputy director,
National Center for Science Education

This book is an essential read for anybody with any interest in what goes on in science education in our schools. Drawing from a lifetime of scholarship, he shows how we got to where we are today, and then, how that is failing the overwhelming majority of our children. He offers a new innovative vision of how to do justice to science and to young people.

Jonathan Osborne, Graduate School of Education,
Stanford University

Science has been seen as both the cause and the solution to every American dilemma for the past sixty years. In *Why We Teach Science*, John L. Rudolph pushes beyond the clichés of those debates to offer a unique, clear-eyed prescription for the kind of science education we really need.

Adam Laats, author of *Fundamentalist*
U and *Creationism USA*.

In *Why We Teach Science*, John Rudolph reflects on Americans' distressing lack of understanding of how science creates reliable knowledge, so starkly revealed by the pandemic. Building on the wisdom of visionaries like Carl Sagan and James Rutherford, he argues convincingly for a new type of science education that focuses on having students learn "where science sits as a knowledge-producing institution in society and the value scientific expertise offers." Beautifully written, Rudolph correctly challenges our long-standing focus on teaching science facts. Badly needed are thousands of college professors to lead the way by addressing this urgent call.

Bruce Alberts, Chancellor's Leadership Chair in Biochemistry and Biophysics for Science and Education, University of California, San Francisco

What goals should science education aim for? And are today's schools achieving those goals? *Why We Teach Science* provides a lucid and comprehensive framework for thinking about these questions, outlining a practical philosophy for science education while also persuasively arguing that some goals are more worth achieving than others.

Andrew Shtulman, Professor of Psychology, Occidental College, author of *Scienceblind*

JOHN L. RUDOLPH

University of Wisconsin-Madison

WHY WE TEACH SCIENCE (AND WHY WE SHOULD)

OXFORD
UNIVERSITY PRESS

Great Clarendon Street, Oxford, OX2 6DP,
United Kingdom

Oxford University Press is a department of the University of Oxford.
It furthers the University's objective of excellence in research, scholarship,
and education by publishing worldwide. Oxford is a registered trade mark of
Oxford University Press in the UK and in certain other countries

© John Rudolph 2023

The moral rights of the author have been asserted

Impression: 1

Published in the United States of America by Oxford University Press
198 Madison Avenue, New York, NY 10016, United States of America

British Library Cataloguing in Publication Data

Data available

Libray of Congress Control Number: 2022942572

ISBN 978–0–19–286719–3

DOI: 10.1093/oso/9780192867193.001.0001

Printed and bound by
CPI Group (UK) Ltd, Croydon, CR0 4YY

PREFACE

One of the benefits of being immersed in the history of science education, as I've been for the past thirty years, is the perspective it gives you. It has enabled me to appreciate the variety of ways science can be taught and the reasons why many felt it should be taught at various times in our history. As a practicing science educator, that history has continually pushed me to rethink what the purpose of science education should be in the present moment, given all the challenges we face in this world. I would add that these thoughts aren't just idle musings. Every fall, a new cohort of aspiring science teachers shows up in my science teaching methods course, ready to hear what I have to say about what should be happening in our middle and high school science classrooms around the country.

From the beginning, I realized that these students already come in with a pretty good idea of what they think science teaching should be about. Of course, they are polite and have always been willing to listen to my thoughts on the subject. But they've all just finished their own rigorous courses of study in the sciences, with some even having earned master's degrees and PhDs. The science-education experiences they've all gone through inevitably have molded their visions of what science teaching should look like. It's not surprising that they talk about teaching the high-level concepts and theories they've mastered, getting students excited about science, and preparing them for STEM careers—or at least getting them ready for the AP courses and the science they'll likely encounter in college. After all, this is the world they know. It's the very educational space that got *them* excited about science and in which they thrived.

Recurring media reports about low student achievement in science and shortages of scientists, engineers, and other technical workers have, undoubtedly, further reinforced their views about science education. And when they turned their attention to consider science teaching as a possible career, many sought out and read science-education standards and policy documents that have repeated the conventional wisdom that higher student achievement in science and more scientists are essential for the country's future. Given the science-related challenges that have risen all around us recently, the science-education world they've come from seems to make even more sense to them. They firmly believe that the next generation needs to know more science— more facts, concepts, and theories—if we hope to preserve our way of life and thrive in the future.

These are the students who file into my classroom every year. And knowing what I know about the science education of the past, current research on science teaching and learning, and how the public engages with science, it became clear to me that my job shouldn't be to provide these aspiring teachers with the latest pedagogical techniques to improve science learning or tricks to spark the interest of apathetic students. I realized that what I needed to do was help them rethink what the purpose of teaching science should be—to consider the experiences and needs of the students who will soon show up in their own science classrooms, most of whom won't have had the school science experiences they did and aren't going to end up in science careers (or maybe aren't going to college even). What do *these* students—the future citizens of our world—need from a middle or high school science class? And so, I began to jot down notes for this book as I developed and revised the readings and activities for my methods class each year.

All of this wasn't merely an academic exercise. As my two daughters grew up and entered high school, I saw firsthand what science education looked like from their perspective. We had more than one conversation about why it was important for them to learn things like the stages of mitosis and meiosis and how to solve gas-law problems. I fell into a tutoring mindset out of long habit as a science teacher and knowing that they "needed" good grades and would likely have to take science courses in college, so it made sense to prepare for those things as much as possible. But such experiences only increased the tensions I felt between why we *say* we teach science, what students learn, and what those learning outcomes *actually do for us*—for my daughters, of course, but for society as well. This book is the culmination of all these professional and personal experiences.

I have incurred many debts along the way and have many people to thank who have directly and indirectly contributed to this book. I've learned much over the years from a wide variety of science-education scholars, including, in no particular order, Rick Duschl, Mark Windschitl, Noah Weeth-Feinstein, Sherry Southerland, Heidi Carlone, John Settlage, Greg Kelly, Andy Zucker, Kip Ault, Jonathan Osborne, Troy Sadler, Stephen Norris, Jim Ryder, Mike Ford, Leema Berland, Rosemary Russ, Peter Hewson, Angelo Collins, Prayas Sutar, and Shusaku Horibe. Special thanks, as always, to Jim Stewart, who made this all happen from the very beginning. On the historical side of the ledger, I'm grateful for the insights provided by David Labaree, Sevan Terzian, Adam Nelson, Herbert Kliebard, David Kaiser, and Bill Reese, whose company and counsel has been and continues to be much appreciated.

I also offer heartfelt thanks to my friends and colleagues who took the time to read and provide feedback on various parts of the manuscript. Among this brave group were Sam Evans, Ryan Batkie, Mark Chandler, Stephanie Whitehorse (for at least showing interest), Doug Larkin, David Meshoulam, Rich Halverson, Mark Olson, Matthew Hora, Andrew Shtulman, Bill Sandoval, and all the students in my fall 2021 science teaching methods course. Any errors or confusions remaining in the book are, of course, mine and mine alone.

I am grateful for financial support from a National Academy of Education/Spencer Foundation Postdoctoral Fellowship, a Spencer Foundation Small Grant, the Graduate School and the Wisconsin Center for Education Research at the University of Wisconsin–Madison, and the National Science Foundation (Grant SES-0114542). Thanks as well to my department chair, Erica Halverson, for her continued support of my work. I'm especially grateful for a much needed post-department-chair semester leave that my Dean, Diana Hess, provided in the spring of 2021 that enabled me to get the bulk of the writing done for this project. She's the best.

Finally, this book couldn't have been written without the support of my wife and life partner, Jen, for whom I am forever grateful for so many things (reading portions of the book being the least of these), and all those conversations and tutoring sessions that I have had over the years with my daughters Audrey and Lydia. As much as I may have taught them, they've taught me that there's more to life than grades and test scores and they continue to teach me more than they realize every day.

JOHN L. RUDOLPH
Madison, Wisconsin

CONTENTS

INTRODUCTION

Science doesn't sit very comfortably in American society. Some of us believe that it's the foundation of social progress and national security. They worry that we aren't doing enough to support it, that we are failing to invest in research that will improve our lives and spur innovation to compete with our adversaries around the globe for military and economic dominance. Others are convinced that science is leading the country astray, believing that scientists routinely push suspect medical treatments on the public, make politically biased recommendations, or, in the case of global warming, have engineered a hoax of proportions never before seen. Science often seems trapped in a never-ending game of king-of-the-hill with advocates forever boosting science toward the top—seeking to expand its status and influence inch by inch—and skeptics trying equally hard to knock it down in the eyes of the public. It's an odd relationship to be sure.

The cultural struggle over the place of science in our lives isn't new. There have always been science boosters among us. The truth is that nearly 75 percent of the public is firmly behind science, believing that its benefits outweigh any harms.[1] But there have always been detractors too. Long before the climate-change and COVID-vaccine skeptics, there were the anti-vaccination societies in the late nineteenth century, opposition to science in the 1930s based on its perceived immorality, and a prominent anti-drinking-water-fluoridation movement in the 1950s, among others.[2]

It seems that the detractors have gotten the upper hand of late, so much so that as I walk my dog around my neighborhood, I regularly pass yard signs proclaiming that "science is real!" Hasn't it always been? Perhaps. But we've never had a time quite like the present in which leading political figures and prominent celebrities and athletes have openly questioned some of the most basic scientific truths about the world. It's one thing to have a vocal group of evangelicals pressure the local school board or state textbook-adoption committee to include some reference to intelligent design in the biology classroom, as has happened routinely over the years. But it's something entirely different, it seems to me, to suggest that the Earth is actually flat or to claim that the coronavirus pandemic is some sort of whole-cloth liberal fabrication. The public marginalization or even complete dismissal of scientific knowledge appears to have reached a new, rather alarming level that has the potential to result in—in fact, *has* resulted in—significant public harm.[3]

Some officials and policy experts fault the low levels of scientific literacy among the general public for the dire state of affairs.[4] And it's true that international assessments, such as the Programme for International Student Assessment (PISA) and the Trends in International Mathematics and Science Study (TIMSS), show American students underperforming their peers around the globe. The nation's report card—the National Assessment of Educational Progress (NAEP)—highlights our lackluster performance in science from one grade level to the next, and surveys of adult content knowledge reported by the National Science Board reveal the poverty of our collective science understanding (only 48 percent of Americans, for example, know whether an electron is larger or smaller than an atom).[5]

The go-to solution for all of this is typically more science education, better science education, or some combination of the two. The United States, in fact, appears to have unwavering faith in the power of science teaching to address any manner of public problem or concern. Worries about the state of the country's science preparation led not too long ago to the passage of the America COMPETES Act in 2007 that called for the recruitment of 10,000 new science and mathematics teachers annually and dramatic increases in both the number of Advanced-Placement science teachers and students successfully completing such courses. Agencies such as the National Science Foundation, the National Institutes of Health, and the Department of Education annually devote millions of dollars to science-education research. And states spend scarce tax dollars developing assessments and academic standards that draw from a long line of science-education policy documents, including those drafted by the American Association for the Advancement of Science's Project 2061, the National Research Council's National Science Education Standards, and the Next Generation Science Standards (NGSS).[6]

We shower all this attention on science education because we believe it provides us with a remarkable suite of social benefits. It's argued that science education is key to the development of new technologies that drive the nation's material prosperity. It readies students for science careers, which is good not only for our economy but also for the students who can set off along a sure pathway to well-paying jobs and a solidly middle-class life. It provides all of us, even those who end up not pursuing technical careers, with a foundational understanding of basic science concepts that is essential to appreciate the vital work scientists do, that enables us to participate in democratic decision-making about pressing science-related social issues, that helps us recognize disinformation and quackery so that we can function more effectively in our daily lives, and that leads us to a richer understanding of the humanistic achievement of science as a way of thinking that has remade the world for the benefit of everyone. What's not to like?

There clearly is no shortage of reasons for teaching science in schools. But these reasons haven't always been with us. Each of them appeared at a particular point in the past, the products of unique social and political contexts from one era in American history to the next. Over time, the individual arguments for science teaching, rather than displacing those that came before, have accumulated into a mass of virtues and justifications, all of which we seem to have accepted without question. Today these arguments for the benefits of science study are treated as self-evident or offered up as a matter of common sense. Indeed, it seems that there isn't anything that a sound understanding of science can't accomplish—and for all students, regardless of their backgrounds, interests, or likely educational or vocational destinations.

Yet, for all the claimed benefits, we never quite seem to fully realize any of them. Economists, business leaders, and politicians continually complain about the persistent need for more scientists and engineers, and the National Science Board assessments of public understanding show that we still can't quite get more than half of the public to know that atoms are in fact much larger than electrons. The growing level of science denial all around us seems to speak for itself about the quality of science teaching in our schools.

Some might insist that all this points to a science-education crisis, which would be tremendously concerning if it weren't for the fact that we *always* seem to be in a science-education crisis. From the Soviet launch of Sputnik in 1957 to the present, there have been recurrent periods of "crisis" every other decade or so that have led to multiple curriculum reforms or the development of standards and then revised standards and then a "next generation" of science standards. We work and work at making science education better, but we never seem to get to where we really want to go in all this.[7]

What if the problem—the reason we never seem to reach our goals—isn't that we're not trying hard enough or spending enough money, but that we haven't really thought carefully about the goals we're trying to reach. I remember watching television with my father when I was growing up. This was before the era of wall-mounted, flat-panel displays, when the TV was a box filled with tubes and switches that sat on an aluminum stand in the corner of the room. When the picture would begin to flicker out, he would walk over and hit the side of the set with his hand hoping to jar the picture back to normal. Sometimes it would work, and sometimes it wouldn't, but that was all he ever tried. A TV repair person might have opened the set up to see what exactly wasn't working, would look at how all those internal parts actually are supposed to work together to produce a quality picture, do a test or two, and proceed to fix what was wrong. When it comes to science education, maybe more science, more standards, more AP course offerings, and more testing isn't the answer; maybe all we're doing is hitting the side of the TV again and again, hoping we get the outcome that advocates have been promising us since science was introduced into schools way back in the nineteenth century.

It may be that science education can't really provide all the benefits we think it can. Perhaps the best way forward is to take a look inside the box—at how students really learn and how they actually use science in their daily lives. This might enable us to get a better handle on what science education can reasonably accomplish for the majority of students in high schools and middle schools in the United States. I'd like to think of this book as doing something of this sort, laying out a practical philosophy of science education for the general reader. It asks what the aims of science education should be, not in the abstract, magical-thinking way that we've approached science education for too long in this country, but rather knowing what we know about how science education typically happens in schools, what the relationship between science and the public is in our present moment, how science education actually contributes to the science and technology workforce and the country's economic growth, and how citizens, in fact, reason about problems and issues they come to face in personal and societal settings.

I begin by tracing the historical origins and transformations of the key arguments for making science a central part of the school curriculum. Although the "aims of science education" have been sliced and packaged a variety of ways by different writers at different times, I've settled on four more or less distinct reasons that have been given over the years for teaching science: (1) studying science leads to an important kind of *cultural appreciation*; (2) it can foster *better general-thinking skills*; (3) the science content knowledge learned is *inherently useful* (what I call the "utility" goal) for the student as well as the nation; and (4) it is essential for *democratic decision-making*.

The cultural appreciation, better thinking, and democratic decision-making reasons fall into the broader aim of what I call *science for general education*. The utility goal—particularly when concerned with national defense or economic growth—can be placed into what I'm calling the category of *technical training*, that is, science education for making future scientists or technical workers.

Each of these arguments has followed its own historical trajectory, shifting over the years in emphasis and form in response to new ideas, significant events, and changing societal needs. There was never a time when only one or two of these arguments held sway; they often appeared together as science-education advocates made their case for this or that type of science teaching, and at times they've become entangled with one another and have blurred into a composite. But I think these four arguments (or justifications or benefits—I use these terms somewhat interchangeably) provide a useful overview and an answer to the—"Why We Teach Science"—portion of the book's title. These are the reasons why society has invested so much time and energy into science education for all members of society.

In the rest of the book, I look at the research and marshal the empirical evidence to assess these reasons and guide my own recommendations. This is the "and Why We Should" part of the story. Some readers—science-education researchers, experts in science communication, educational psychologists, and learning scientists—will be familiar with the material in these chapters. This book isn't for them (though perhaps they might benefit from the bigger picture I sketch). It's for the interested public—the school-board members, scientists, teachers, textbook authors, parents, policymakers, and thought leaders who are primarily responsible for creating and implementing the science education our children experience each and every day in schools across the nation. This book is an effort to bring what we know about how science is learned and used to those readers, to explode the myths and assumptions that have for too long shaped the teaching of science in our high schools and middle schools (and even in the introductory science courses in our colleges and universities).

The main points I make in the second half are, first, that the argument for utility—which I frame as the ongoing desire for technical training in this country as it pertains to national goals—doesn't come close to meeting the needs of the majority of students in our schools nor of society more broadly. The focus (particularly at the secondary level), I argue, should be on teaching science for general education, that is, science for the non-scientist. The aim of this type of teaching is to achieve what many refer to as "scientific literacy" (a phrase that turns out to be not at all helpful in thinking carefully about what we hope science education might accomplish). I then walk the reader through what researchers know about how people interact with and use science in the real world and end with recommendations that emphasize the *democratic decision-making* argument for science education. Central to realizing this goal, I argue, is understanding the need to build new levels of public trust in science and its institutions. Based on what we know, this is the goal most worth pursuing and that we can actually achieve. Achieving this goal gives us the best hope of resolving the central challenge we currently face—productively engaging with scientific expertise in our decentralized, democratic political system.

Ultimately, the main thrust of this book concerns the legitimacy of our stated purposes for teaching science now and throughout the history of schooling in the United States. In this current—some might say dangerous—social and political moment when the authority of science is under attack, we can ill afford an educational system or approach to science education that is only thinly supported philosophically, logically, and empirically. In other words, when it comes to teaching science, we should know what we are seeking to accomplish and have a reasonably good sense that the curricular materials and pedagogical methods we employ are likely to actually work. Without that, at a minimum, we open ourselves as educators and citizens to the further undermining of science as a public good and consigning ourselves to living in a world governed by passion and power and greed rather than by intelligence.

PART 1

WHAT WE SAY

CHAPTER 1

THE REASONS WE TEACH SCIENCE

Science Education for Culture

Few things display the cultural argument for science as well as the old PBS television series *Cosmos*. On Sunday evenings in the fall of 1980, Cornell University astronomer and science popularizer Carl Sagan took viewers on an epic tour through space and time—a tour not only through the vast expanse of the universe, but through our human past, the recorded history of which spanned only the briefest flash in the last seconds of a hypothetical cosmic year. "We're about to begin a journey through the cosmos," Sagan says in the opening scene. "We'll encounter galaxies, and suns, and planets, life and consciousness coming into being, evolving and perishing. Worlds of ice and stars of diamond. Atoms as massive as suns and universes smaller than atoms." The award-winning series, which ran for thirteen episodes from September through December, explored among its many topics the evolutionary history of life on Earth, the Big Bang theory of creation, the life cycles of stars, the greenhouse effect, and animal intelligence. All of it inspired awe. "The cosmos," in Sagan's soaring rhetoric, "is full beyond measure of elegant truths of exquisite interrelationships of the awesome machinery of nature."[1]

But his story wasn't just about the wonders of the physical universe—it was also a story about us: "how we achieved our present understanding of the cosmos, how the cosmos has shaped our evolution and our culture, and what our fate may be." As Sagan tells it, our ability to make sense of the deep complexity of that machinery, that, in itself, is a thing of true wonder. "Our contemplations of the cosmos stir us," he explains; they trigger a profound emotional response in those seeking to understand. "There is a tingling in the spine, a catch in the voice, a faint sensation: as if a distant memory of falling from a great height." With those opening lines, Sagan shared with the audience (one that would grow to over 400 million viewers across sixty countries) both the beauty of nature itself *and* the amazing accomplishment of the human intellect to make sense of it all through science.[2]

The cultural goals of science education have always centered on these twin targets—the appreciation of the wonders of the natural world and of the human species' ability to grasp its subtle complexities. The two have long been entwined and are inevitably defined in relation to one another. We strive to understand the operations of nature and, in doing so, come to understand our own place in the natural order; making sense of the cosmos (to borrow Sagan's phrase) helps us know ourselves.

But our ability as a species to discover and know the universe around us, in this argument, depends on the operations of a particular collection of individuals in modern society—the scientists. And their community has its own set of norms and culture derived from ideas about progress grounded in human reason and the evidence of our senses. Teaching about science, then, enables learners to come to understand and appreciate how scientists specifically engage in the process of discovering things about the world and how a particular set of values guides that process.

Teaching science for culture—to understand and appreciate the wonders of the universe, the place of humankind within that universe, and how scientists and the scientific community work to develop those understandings—is perhaps the most foundational of all the goals of science education. It goes back to the very beginning of science teaching in Western civilization and has served as one of the key justifications at all levels, from elementary school up through university. The prevalence of this argument has varied over the years, going as far back as the early 1800s, but its presence—in its continued affirmation of the power of human reason to make sense of the material world—has been constant in calls for science education up to the present day.

One of the earliest arguments for science, or the study of the natural world, as a means of cultural appreciation came from the realm of natural theology. This way of thinking about science, which was popular in the early nineteenth century, emphasized exploring the origin and workings of the physical and biological world for the evidence it provided of the divine. Society then was immersed in a cultural framework of Christian belief, and the idea of God as the designer of all things was central to this belief system. One could bring glory to the Creator through the careful study of his handiwork, so the argument went. Science was thus justified by its ability to affirm this worldview and foster greater appreciation for the beneficence of God.[3]

Natural theology was a standard subject of university study in England through the mid-1800s. It served as a unifying framework for scientific work in the United States as well during that time.[4] From this perspective, the cultural goal of science instruction was all about placing man within the divine order of things, along with fostering an appreciation of God's work. The Harvard naturalist Louis Agassiz explained this in an 1859 talk he gave at the New York State House in Albany, where he was invited to comment on the importance of teaching science in schools as a means of realizing this goal. It was through the study of nature, he said, that we can "become better acquainted with ourselves." It allows us "to know how we are related to the whole animal kingdom." It might seem preposterous to compare a man to a fish, he said as an example, "and yet the two are constructed on the same plan." "The same elements of structure which we may see in the fish are, only in a more lofty combination, presented again in the man." It was clear to Agassiz (and most other naturalists back then) that such continuity was evidence of the hand of God and that science teaching would naturally reinforce this Christian worldview.[5]

As science gained in prestige and professionalism in the second half of the nineteenth century, the cultural goal of science teaching shifted away from the spiritual to the accomplishments of science as a field and the scientists themselves. Science grew in popularity in the second half of the nineteenth century in the United States. Its advocates increasingly touted the new theories that provided secular explanations of the many wonders of nature and the universe. The law of conservation of energy and theories of light and biological evolution—following the publication of Charles Darwin's *On the Origin of Species* (1859) and *The Descent of Man* (1871)—all seemed to offer materialistic accounts of previously mysterious natural phenomena.

The educated elite attended lectures, purchased magazines, and generally consumed science in large measure both because it was interesting and because it had become the thing to do—engaging with science in these ways had become a marker of high culture. They flocked to talks given across the country by the British natural philosopher John Tyndall in 1872 on the nature of light and the importance of science in society as well as those by the biologist T. H. Huxley in 1876 on evolution, the history of life on Earth, and appreciating humankind's place in nature.[6] The writer and editor E. L. Youmans, one of the most influential American science popularizers of the time, published a collection of essays (written by scientific luminaries such as Tyndall, Huxley, Michael Faraday, John Herschel, and others) in a volume titled *The Culture Demanded by Modern Life* in 1867 that called for a greater focus on science education in the schools and colleges. Youmans followed this with the launch of his International Science Series of books and the widely circulated magazine *Popular Science Monthly,* all of which brought new ideas in science to a wider and wider audience. Science and the scientific worldview, it seemed to these thinkers, was simply the best way to approach and appreciate the natural world and human society within it.[7]

In the early 1900s, American textbook authors increasingly included biographies of eminent scientists to foster student appreciation of the human element of scientific progress. They included tales and portraits of scientific greats such as Newton, Galileo, Darwin, Faraday, Dalton, and others that highlighted their unique backgrounds along with the theoretical and experimental contributions they made to their respective disciplines. It was an attempt to capture student interest in science following the recommendations of psychologists of the time such as G. Stanley Hall, who argued that "boys in their teens have a veritable passion for the stories of great men." Physics, for example, "has its saints and martyrs and devotees, its dramatic incidents and epochs, its struggles with superstition, its glorious triumphs," he explained. All this gives "a present sense of achievement and progress, and nothing appeals to the young more than to feel vividly the sense of growth." The message to students was clear—here were the heroes of science to look up to on whose shoulders the new culture of a scientific world was being built.[8]

The efforts to push for a greater appreciation of science came from a growing sense that the ideas of science were profoundly shaping human culture. As more and more students began attending public schools across the nation, advocates of science teaching felt that a broad exposure to the knowledge of the natural world science had uncovered was essential to a proper education rather than the more specialized training designed for the few who would go on in the sciences. Survey courses that aimed to provide as much general information as possible about the student's local environment were, in fact, often referred to as "culture courses" (rather than disciplinary courses). Those encouraging such an approach looked back fondly on the popularization efforts of the great scientists of the nineteenth century—"Davy, Faraday, Tyndall, Pasteur, Humboldt, Maxwell, Huxley, Agassiz, Cooke, Shaler, and the like; for these men all preached the doctrine that science is good for culture and should be given to all."[9]

By the early 1930s, science educators in the United States fully embraced the cultural goal of science teaching. The National Society for the Study of Education (NSSE), an organization of influential educators and policymakers, offered an in-depth look at the goals of science education in its 1932 yearbook. "This is an age of science," one contributor wrote, "first in the sense that present modes of living are possible only because of contributions that have come from this field, and second, in the sense that the principles that guide our thinking have been enormously influenced by contributions from the work of scientists." In such an age, the public needed to understand that the comforts of modern living—that came from the control of energy, improvements in health and sanitation, and mastery of the food supply—were the direct fruits of scientific work. Science, moreover, had freed people from "the bondage of superstition and from the shackles of necromancy, alchemy, witchcraft, astrology, and other errors of understanding." Science, in other words, had made the world of that time, and the primary goal of science education was to ensure the public recognized and understood its influence and power.[10]

This push to establish science as the predominant way to live and see the world rose to the fore in the 1920s and 1930s. Some even called for science to take its place as the foundation of an alternate religion known as humanism, a system of belief that exalted scientific thought and insisted on human reason as a new, living worldview and the only effective means for solving societal problems. Unlike natural theology, which sought to provide evidence for the Christian interpretation of man and nature, scientific humanism dispensed with notions of the divine entirely. Its advocates (including individuals such as John Dewey, Albert Einstein, and Julian Huxley, grandson of T. H. Huxley) insisted that the only way to deal with the practical concerns of the world was through science and its methods. Appeals to the supernatural could be dispensed with as a source of truth and values. Science provided a better, universal way to make sense of everyday experience and promised to serve as the ultimate lever for social progress.[11]

World War II contributed even more to the growing status of science as a result of the dramatic contributions it made to the fight (the most notable of these being the atomic bomb). However, scientists felt that it was a status based on a misunderstanding. Thrust into the postwar public spotlight, they increasingly confronted an audience they felt had only a limited grasp of their work, an audience that believed science was only good for producing wonderous—sometimes terrifying—gadgets and technologies. Such perceptions increasingly seemed to push scientists away from the public into their isolated laboratories, places the average citizen struggled to connect with. This estrangement spurred some scientists to launch an educational project that they hoped would result in a greater appreciation of the role of science in an increasingly technological society that would finally allow for its full integration into public life.

This postwar education project, which extended at its height from the end of the war through the 1990s, sought to show the public that science involved more than the mere production of technologies for improving the material conditions of life, but was instead, at its core, a quest for understanding—an intellectual endeavor focused on answering the ultimate questions of the natural world and the place of humans within it. Such work was valuable, of course, for the practical applications that inevitably would spin off of such research. The essence of that work, though—the drive to understand and explain nature through the application of rational thought—scientists believed, had intrinsic value of the highest order. The public appreciation of that value, they felt, would require a fundamental cultural shift in American society, but one that was essential for science to survive and flourish.

The efforts that best capture this push for cultural understanding after the war took place at Harvard University. There Harvard president (and research chemist) James Conant began an innovative undergraduate program in general science education. As outlined in the landmark 1945 report *General Education in a Free Society* (commonly referred to as the Harvard Redbook in reference to the color of its binding), the new program included courses aimed specifically at the non-specialist, those who would become "lawyers, writers, teachers, politicians, public servants, and businessmen."[12] Science taught from this perspective, according to the report, "should be characterized mainly by broad integrative elements—the comparison of scientific with other modes of thought, the comparison and contrast of the individual sciences with one another, the relations of science with its own past and with general human history, and of science with problems of human society."[13]

Conant's specific contribution to science teaching in this program was a course he developed that he and others taught to Harvard undergraduates from the mid-1940s through the 1960s. It employed case studies from the history of science that illustrated how early scientists formulated and refined scientific ideas as a result of their interactions with the world around them. Such a treatment, Conant noted, in harmony with the Redbook prescriptions, would ideally include the examination of the interactions between science and society and, in addition, "can hardly ignore completely the influence of new scientific concepts on contemporary thinking about the structure of the universe of the nature and destiny of man." All this was to be in service to the larger goal Conant envisioned of "assimilating science into our secular culture."[14]

The assimilation Conant hoped for was nowhere on the immediate horizon, however. Concerns over the growing isolation of science from mainstream culture intensified during the 1950s with the arrival of the Red Scare—which often targeted scientists as potentially subversive—and the rise of a general climate of anti-intellectualism across the country, which denigrated the very nature of scientific work. By the end of the decade, the chasm between science and other systems of knowing appeared wider than ever and was given voice in C. P. Snow's famous "Two Cultures" talk of 1959. By then, the appearance of the Earth-orbiting artificial satellite Sputnik had accelerated American efforts to bolster the production of scientists and engineers to keep pace with the Soviets. This exacerbated the divide between science and the public and pushed a view of science—as military technology—at odds with the humanistic view many scientists held of their work. Many critics urged a return to humanistic approaches to education to counter the raw technological focus of science at the time. More needed to be done to bridge the cultural divide.[15]

Leading scientists spoke up for greater cultural understanding in response throughout the decade. Nobel Prize-winning physicist I. I. Rabi, for example, worried that the public was too willing to "keep the fearsome fruits but reject the spirit of science" just to keep ahead of the Russians. He explained that "what the scientist really desires is for his science to be understood, to become an integral part of our general culture, to be given proper weight in the cultural and practical affairs of the world." In order to accomplish this, he felt that "the scientists must learn to teach science in the spirit of wisdom and in the light of the history of human thought and human effort."[16] Julius Stratton, the vice-president and provost of MIT, echoed Rabi's statements, arguing that "the education of scientists cannot be isolated from the educational aims and patterns of our population as a whole." It was the education of the population as a whole, in fact, that needed to be infused with science. "There *is* one great unifying force working in our age, and that is science," he declared. "We must turn to science for the *lingua franca* of modern men and find in science the vehicle of modern thought."[17]

Of all the postwar scientists, though, perhaps no one's work did more to embody the cultural goals of science education than that of the physicist Gerald Holton. As a young faculty member at Harvard in the late 1940s, Holton signed on to help develop and teach one of the general-science courses developed as part of the Redbook recommendations. He worked alongside the physicist Edwin Kemble teaching a course focused on the historical influence of physics on philosophy, technology, and society. Materials from that course served as the foundation for a textbook he wrote in 1952, *Introduction to Concepts and Theories in Physical Science*. Holton's goal with the book was to present science "as *experience*, as an integrated and exciting intellectual adventure." Here the culture to be understood was that of the scientists themselves. By presenting science in its historical and philosophical context, the hope was that students not only would see how "a particular idea came to have meaning and importance," but also would appreciate the "sources, motivations, and methods of approach of the founders of science, illustrating the human triumph behind the bare abstractions."[18]

The book found a receptive audience among a good segment of the college physics-teaching community and went through multiple editions and revisions over the next five decades. The last version, published in 2001, was the textbook *Physics, the Human Adventure: From Copernicus to Einstein and Beyond*, revised and updated with the help of the science historian Stephen Brush. The first chapter's opening paragraph clearly spells out the cultural goals the authors had in mind: "Our purpose in this book is to tell the story of the major ideas that have led to our current understanding of how the physical universe functions." "At the same time," they continued, "we also aim to show that the growth of science was part of the general development of our civilization, as it is to this day. We think that you will find it an amazing, even inspiring story of the power of the ideas of men and women who dedicated their lives to the search for truths."[19]

Holton's cultural approach made its way into high school science classrooms as well. Inspired by his 1952 textbook, California high school teacher F. James Rutherford moved to Harvard and teamed up with Holton and science education faculty member Fletcher Watson to produce what came to be called *Project Physics*. The curriculum, pitched at middle-level to upper-level high school students, was widely adopted in American physics classrooms beginning in the early 1970s. It promised a humanistic alternative for students turned off by the more narrowly focused, disciplinary physics courses standard at the time, which many saw as designed only for producing future scientists. In the spirit of Holton's earlier undergraduate general-science course, *Project Physics* ranged much more widely, seeking to show the "tapestry of cross connections" between physics and other knowledge-producing fields such as chemistry, engineering, biology, psychology, literature, and all the various cultural activities of humankind. It told the story about how the ideas of physics emerged and came together historically, a story that would take students, according to Holton, to "a higher vantage point, a more encompassing view of the working nature, of the style of life of the scientist, and of the power of the human mind."[20]

The thread of this particular approach to science education continued unbroken through the 1980s and 1990s in the ongoing professional work of Rutherford. After serving both in the National Science Foundation (NSF) and the Department of Education, he was enlisted in 1981—just months after the successful TV broadcast of Carl Sagan's *Cosmos*—to lead the science-education reform efforts of the American Association for the Advancement of Science. That effort, tabbed Project 2061 (for the year when Halley's Comet would return to the night skies in its orbit around the sun—which provided what Rutherford thought was a long enough period of time to do science education right), aimed to lay out a vision of what every citizen should know about science in that distant future.

Given his past work with Holton and *Project Physics*, it wasn't surprising that Rutherford foregrounded cultural understanding in his vision, which he laid out in the 1989 report *Science for All Americans*. Whatever students might learn in science classrooms, it needed to be material that was "so important in human history or so pervasive in our culture that a general education would be incomplete without them." It should, moreover, provide students with a philosophical foundation, enabling them "to ponder the enduring questions of human meaning such as life and death, perception and reality, the individual good versus the collective welfare, certainty and doubt."[21] The recommendations included teaching "how the universe is put together, how it works," and an appreciation of where humans "fit in the cosmic scheme of things." They highlighted episodes from the history of science—the work of Galileo, Newton, Lyell, Darwin, and others—that were deemed "of surpassing significance to our cultural heritage" and offered new material related to the scientific enterprise to show students, for example, "how the direction of scientific research is affected by informal influences within the culture of science itself" and how science is "built upon a distinctive set of values" that are "increasingly influential in shaping shared cultural values."[22]

The kind of science understanding put forward in Project 2061's *Science for All Americans* nicely encapsulates the major cultural goals of science education that emerged over the past one hundred and fifty years. It showcases the longstanding commitment to learning the content of science—the things that exist and how they work—as a means of appreciating the beauty of the natural world and, more importantly, the place of humankind in the grand scheme of the cosmos. It also illustrates the desire to foster in students a deep appreciation of the human mind and its ability to grasp and order the world out there—to construct a complex edifice of concepts, models, and theories that allow us to make sense of everything around us. That understanding, cultural proponents insist, as it has grown by leaps and bounds over the years, has itself increasingly permeated all facets of our lives, continually reshaping and defining what we know and can do—which, in the faith many have in the good science brings, entails understanding and nourishing the unique culture of science as well. The science of our time has become a part of us, of who we are as a people. Science education for culture is, in the end, an endeavor in self-understanding. An education that neglects this, so this argument goes, is no education at all.

Science Education for Better Thinking

If the *science education for culture* argument is about developing an appreciation of the majesty of the natural world and how science—and the work of scientists—increasingly shapes the larger culture of modern civilization, *science education for better thinking* covers arguments related to the idea that scientific study has the power to bring about various forms of intellectual improvement. Belief in this goal has centered most often on the process rather than the facts or content of science. That is, it has been long claimed by science education advocates that learning how scientists go about creating knowledge or simply engaging in the process itself (in a self-aware manner or not) will result in certain benefits accruing to the individual, benefits that are typically of the cognitive sort.

We can see this in the discussions that took place in the late 1980s among the panel of scientists and experts Jim Rutherford assembled as part of AAAS's Project 2061. The panelists had just gone over a set of draft reports that outlined what students should come away with from their science classes, and Alden Dunham, a program officer from the Carnegie Corporation of New York (the foundation that provided seed money for the project), commented that he was appalled by the things the lay public was willing to believe, "whether it is astrology or witchcraft or what have you." The popularity of astrology in the United States, in particular, had been on the rise and was seen as a clear affront to scientific thinking. "It is basic to the argument of why [Project 2061] is important," Dunham insisted. "The irrational in American life," he went on, is a "frightening phenomenon," and Rutherford concurred, noting that "rational thinking" was critical for "organiz[ing] our lives." Understanding science, the group agreed, was the path toward realizing that goal.[23]

While the participants of Project 2061 believed rational thinking was a key "habit of mind" that a sound education in science could cultivate, in earlier periods that goal might have been called "intellectual power" or, more recently, "critical thinking." And there were (and are) other cognitive goals as well beyond the ability to engage in logical analysis. Among these have been powers of observation, memory, judgment, and—though lying outside the cognitive realm—moral uplift (a goal popular at least for a brief time in the late 1800s). Common to all of these, however poorly or precisely specified, is that the skill or quality, once developed, inheres within the individual student; it becomes a part of their cognitive, perceptual, or moral attributes—attributes that, while refined by scientific practice, have value *outside* of science, in the other facets of one's life. This particular belief—that the doing of science has the power to produce these benefits—has long pushed educators to shape classroom pedagogy in the image of scientific practice, for better and worse.

One of the earliest arguments for science education as a means for better thinking was made in the middle of the nineteenth century. The predominant theory of learning at the time was based on faculty psychology, which entailed the belief that the mind consisted of distinct faculties or capacities that could be strengthened with appropriate types of intellectual exercise or, without exercise, would wither from neglect. This theory was famously articulated in a report issued by the faculty of Yale College in 1828.

Given that the mental faculties were the parts of the mind that took in and processed information, the primary goal of education was to exercise and develop them—to *discipline* the mind—with a secondary goal being to provide the student with up-to-date knowledge, which the Yale report referred to as the *furniture* of the mind—the "facts" one knows.[24] It had long been accepted that studying the classical languages and mathematics was the best method of instilling such mental discipline. Learning Latin and Greek, for example, was thought to train the faculties of memory and judgment most effectively, and the study of mathematics was believed to best develop reasoning. (Years later, one critic referred to this approach dismissively as the "grindstone-theory" of learning, the idea that young minds require a "process of sharpening," and that the instruments for that sharpening were "the grammars of the two dead languages, and the elementary portions of abstract mathematics."[25])

Alongside the growing public fascination with science in the mid-1800s, leading scientists and educators increasingly argued that the study of the sciences was just as if not more effective as Greek, Latin, and mathematics in achieving the desired mental discipline in students. Science education had long been thought to provide only the furniture of the mind—the facts of nature, knowledge of how things worked. But many scientists believed that shifting the emphasis in science teaching to engage students in the *process* of science, primarily via laboratory work, would open the door to the same kind of mental training provided by mathematics and the classical languages. E. L. Youmans made this argument in the opening chapter of *The Culture Demanded by Modern Life* in 1867.[26]

This disciplinary argument for the value of scientific study prevailed for decades. At a meeting of the New York State Science Teachers Association in 1896 (nearly thirty years after Youmans' claims), a presenter invited the audience to "consider *what* faculties of the mind may be developed" by the study of the physical sciences—"what opportunities do these subjects afford for the exercise of the mental powers?" he asked—and then proceeded to list things such as perception, judgment, cultivation of imagination, and induction, which, as a reasoning process, "is best obtained in the laboratory" (along with all the others). As late as 1906, Harvard president Charles Eliot continued to sing the praises of science teaching via the laboratory, noting that it was an ideal way to "train the powers of observation, and what may be called the judgment in inferring, the kind of judgment that is a guide to conduct in this world."[27]

If the power of science education to discipline the mind wasn't enough, many late-nineteenth-century scientists insisted that it had the added benefit of improving morality. Having students come face to face with the immovable facts of nature in the laboratory—the very place from which truths about the natural world were conceived—couldn't help but instill virtue. As the ecologist Stephen Forbes described it, the direct and careful observations of nature "form the steps of the ladder by which the soul may climb from the abyss of mystery, in which it has its origin, to the sublime heights of thought." And the geologist William North Rice noted in the same vein that "no one can become imbued in any measure with the spirit of science—the spirit of unselfish, courageous, reverent truth-seeking—without some degree of moral uplifting." Claims about this moral benefit both traded on the earlier cultural goals tied to natural theology (seeing the divine in nature and knowing one's place within God's creation) and aligned science with the predominantly moral framework of schooling at the time. Students would walk out of their science classrooms not only with their mental skills sharpened but would get a dash of virtue to boot. Hard to argue with that.[28]

Talk about mental discipline and moral improvement largely disappeared in the twentieth century. One reason was that new work in the emerging field of educational psychology had demonstrated fairly convincingly that the mind-as-muscle, faculty psychology theory of learning couldn't pull its own weight. Another reason was that growing school enrollments, the professionalization of education, and the rapid industrialization of the American economy had combined to shift public views about what school should be for. In the first decades of the new century, most children going to school were not headed to college for higher learning. As a result, the new educational psychologists and science educators insisted that school science should be built to engage the natural interests of these less academically inclined students. Instead of training them to master the science disciplines in sterile laboratories, the plan was to teach them to use the scientific method to address problems they encountered in their everyday world. And so, from the late nineteenth century through the first half of the twentieth century, the cognitive goal of teaching science shifted from strengthening the mental faculties to developing problem-solving skills.[29]

This new problem-solving emphasis arrived in schools in a somewhat backward way. The idea originated in a little book that the philosopher and educator John Dewey published in 1910 called *How We Think*. His purpose in writing the book, which was based on his time as a faculty member and head of the laboratory school at the University of Chicago, was to give teachers a guide for organizing their instruction to promote reflective thinking among the students crowding into the nation's classrooms.

He modeled the essence of such thought on the process of science that he observed among his scientist colleagues in Chicago. "I saw they had a method that worked ... the experimental method," he explained to a friend, "hypothesis in control of action," and from that, he abstracted the steps that, he felt, made up every act of thought. There were five: "(i) a felt difficulty; (ii) its location and definition; (iii) suggestion of possible solution; (iv) development by reasoning of the bearings of the suggestion; [and] (v) further observation and experiment leading to its acceptance or rejection; that is, the conclusion of belief or disbelief."[30]

Dewey believed these five steps captured the process the mind went through when confronted with a challenge or puzzling situation. It was meant to be an everyday version of what scientists did in their work. The book became a best-seller, and as it happened, science educators latched onto the five steps not as a general method (borrowed from science) of how people think but rather as an informal description of what scientists did when they did science. It became for them "the scientific method" itself. They quickly refashioned their curricula with Dewey's easily teachable five steps as the central learning goal of science education.

The focus on problem solving and the everyday applications of science bubbled up to the surface of textbooks and classrooms almost immediately following the publication of How We Think and remained prominent all the way through the 1940s. High school science textbooks were filled with examples of how understanding science and its process had led to the solution of the various problems of living and contributed to the progress of civilization. Many of the books provided end-of-chapter activities and projects that asked students to puzzle over problems of home and family life so that they might practice using the scientific method for themselves. As one biology textbook author put it: "The boy or girl of average ability upon admission to secondary school is not a thinking individual;" therefore, biology, which was often the first and only science subject students took, "should be primarily the vehicle by which the child is taught to solve problems and to think straight in doing so."[31] There was even the development of an entirely new course, general science, which had the primary objective of developing problem-solving skills in students in an effort, as the ad copy for one textbook read, to teach students "*how to think consistently, clearly, logically.*"[32]

National policy documents highlighted the problem-solving goal. A report in the 1932 NSSE yearbook, *A Program for Teaching Science,* stated clearly that "in this society man must meet and solve problems," which required that schools provide instruction that, among other things, "exercises methods that have been used in solving problems, and ... that furnishes practice in the use of these methods." The follow-up NSSE yearbook fifteen years later (*Science Education in American Schools*) similarly emphasized the importance of "providing opportunity for growth of skill in the use of the elements of the scientific method," which were defined as the steps identified by Dewey. "Problem-solving behavior" could only be developed if it was "correctly and repeatedly practiced" and "carried over into experiences outside the classroom." The way students were taught problem solving always came back to some version of the five steps from *How We Think.* Dewey, in fact, had become something of a touchstone for all of science education during these years, synonymous with the problem-solving approach to teaching science.[33]

With the onset of World War II, science-education boosters extended their arguments beyond its value for practical problem solving to the broader concept of "critical thinking" in response to the waves of disinformation circulating during the war. By learning to apply the scientific method, the National Committee on Science Teaching wrote in 1942, students "become adept in seeing through propaganda, foolish superstitions, and unscientific procedures." Moreover, "they develop an inquiring mind, [and] acquire the attitudes of open-mindedness and tolerance." "Perhaps the best way in which to summarize the scientific method," the committee concluded, "is say that it is critical thinking." It was well known that engaging in science contributed to key abilities such as "observation, evaluation, experimentation, [and] rational interpretation" (echoes of faculty psychology perhaps). But these, the committee explained, all served as the foundation for critical thinking—"critical thinking should serve as the climax." The equation was clear: the scientific method equaled critical thinking; and critical thinking equaled better thinking; and, in the words of the committee, "better thinking results in better living."[34]

Studies of the human mind and its thought processes gained renewed attention during the 1950s and 1960s as the interdisciplinary field of cognitive psychology coalesced around the work of Jerome Bruner, Jacqueline Goodnow, George Austin, George Miller, and others. Their studies of human mental processes drew on scientific thinking as a model for human thinking (not unlike Dewey) and explored the importance of elements such as creativity, intuition, modeling, and invention in the thought process. Prescriptions for science teaching rapidly incorporated these new ideas. The last of the NSSE yearbooks devoted to science education, aptly titled *Rethinking Science Education*, published in 1960, explicitly discussed the ways that creativity and scientific attitudes might work together to further the aim of teaching critical-thinking skills (which could be thought of as interchangeable with the concepts of "scientific method" and "problem solving").[35]

Science was both the means for achieving these better-thinking outcomes (through its study and students' engagement in the process) and the model for all rational thought. This view was put forward emphatically in a 1966 report by the Educational Policies Commission, an influential policy group assembled by the National Education Association. The report, *Education and the Spirit of Science,* was a love song to the scientific worldview. "In the modern world," the authors began, "the approach of rational inquiry—the mode of thought which underlies science and technology—is spreading rapidly and, in the process, is changing the world in profound ways." As such, it was crucial that schools play a central role in promoting the "values on which science is everywhere based," which included a longing to know and understand, the questioning of all things, the search for data, demand for verification, respect for logic, and consideration of the premises and consequences in reasoning.[36] "What is being advocated here is not the production of more physicists, biologists, or mathematicians," the commission noted, "but rather the development of persons whose approach to life as a whole is that of a person who thinks—a rational person." The values of scientific thought, in this view, would become the values of human rationality.[37]

Bringing things closer to the present, arguments for better thinking have turned toward less high-minded and more practical goals related to effective workplace performance. A committee of the National Research Council (NRC) in 2010 explored how science education might contribute to so-called "twenty-first-century skills" deemed necessary for the jobs of the future, skills such as adaptability, complex communication, nonroutine problem solving, self-management and development, and systems thinking. These skills had been identified as increasingly valuable in an era of greater automation across employment sectors. Although many researchers are less likely now to subscribe to the view that scientific thinking immediately or easily transfers to non-science contexts, the NRC committee found potential nonetheless for school-based scientific-inquiry activities (suitably designed and implemented) to promote the generalized workforce skills in question. In this case, while scientific thinking is no longer held to be the sole model for all that's cognitively good, engaging students in science remains at the top of the list of activities that seem to promote desirable thinking outcomes.[38]

Over the years, claims that the study of science or, more often, that actually doing science contributes to better thinking have remained a constant feature of science-education talk. Whether it was a belief that careful observation and reasoning during laboratory work in the late 1800s exercised the mental faculties of students, or that memorizing and following the steps of the scientific method in science classrooms honed student problem-solving skills for everyday use, or that the immersion of students in inquiry or project-based science activities contributed to the development of some sort of greater rationality or generalizable workplace skills in whatever century, the common denominator in every historical period has been the belief that science education (properly experienced) provided students with some set of cognitive skills or abilities that had value out in the everyday, non-scientific world. In each instance—whatever the underlying psychological theory—advocates have assumed that science education was never just for learning science, but rather equally (or more so) for the development of the skills and capacities of the individual.

Science Education for Utility—Personal Use, National Security, and Economic Growth

Knowledge is power, as they say, and far and away the most compelling case for science education has been that understanding how the world works enables us to get things done. The "facts" of science (the "furniture" of the mind in the old faculty-psychology view) have always been valued for the control they've given us over our surroundings. Such knowledge has been referred to variously as useful, utilitarian, functional, instrumental, or practical. When science courses such as chemistry, physics, and biology first appeared in schools and colleges, they were often called "information" subjects (in contrast to the "disciplinary" subjects of mathematics and the classical languages), and the information they provided was seen as useful in successfully conducting the affairs of life. By learning about mechanical advantage, you could build a more powerful machine. Knowing the conditions under which bacteria thrive and multiply made for food-processing techniques that prevented spoilage. Scientific knowledge was and is the foundation of countless technologies that allow us to shape the world to fit our needs; it enables us to anticipate the consequences of our actions. It is, simply, extremely useful.

While the utilitarian argument has always been present, the focus of that argument has changed over the years—sometimes dramatically. Science was introduced into American schools in the nineteenth century almost exclusively for its practical value (claims about its ability to discipline the mind came later). The emphasis was initially on the use of science for national development before shifting to its value for the individual, an emphasis that persisted through the mid-twentieth century. The onset of World War II led to an emphasis on science education for national security as the Cold War with the Soviet Union ramped up. This was followed by calls for science education to help fight the economic stagnation in the 1970s and 1980s as American businesses competed with emerging industrial powers overseas. All this is to say that the utilitarian argument can be found in essentially three flavors since the mid-1800s—science education for *personal use, national security*, and *economic growth.*

On the surface, these uses of science seem radically different from one another. Yet, in all these instances—whether scientific knowledge helped a farmer bring products to market in the 1800s, a homeowner heat their house in the 1930s, a team of scientists develop advanced radar technologies during the war, or engineers build better fiber-optic connectivity and, thus, ensure rising stock prices for tech companies in the 2000s—science education has been seen as the lever for positive change. Teaching students the facts, concepts, and theories of the natural world, so this argument goes, enables them to get things done for the benefit of themselves, their communities, and the nation. The belief that science produces "practical" knowledge has always been a selling point for science education, most recently because of the literal "cash value" it seems to promise in terms of economic growth. It's what makes the world go.

Personal Utility

As far back as 1889, the eminent ecologist Stephen Forbes explained that the driving reason for the emphasis on science in schools "was really the *practical.*" As he stated in his presidential address to the Illinois State Teachers' Association then, these subjects "were added to the public school course because it was hoped . . . that the lot of the countryman and of the workmen in towns would be ameliorated if they knew more of the facts and laws of matter and of life."[39] Science education, in other words, was seen as a means to make life easier for the average person. In the 1920s and 1930s, the focus of education generally turned more toward individual student interests, and science education was increasingly sold primarily as a means for meeting personal needs. A group of reformers put forward a somewhat radical plan for the science curriculum in 1920 that foregrounded these individual goals over the traditional content of the science subjects. These new goals included promoting health, worthy home membership, preparation for work, and the effective use of leisure time.[40]

In each of these areas, the practical value of science to the individual seemed clear. The relevance to health was obvious—"the control and elimination of disease, the provision of adequate hospital facilities and medical inspection, the maintenance of public health, all necessitate widely disseminated knowledge and practice of the basic principles of personal hygiene and public sanitation." Scientific knowledge was essential in the home not only for the homemaker and those responsible for childcare, but to family members "who may be called upon to make repairs to the heating and ventilating system, to adjust the electrical appliances, or to perform any of the many services that make for an effective home." In the area of vocational preparation, "courses in shop physics, applied electricity, physics of the home, industrial and household chemistry, applied biological sciences, physiology, and hygiene will be of value to many students." And science was seen as valuable even in the pursuit of leisure. Knowing the principles of optics and something of the chemical processes of film development, for example, would make one a better photographer.[41]

Otis Caldwell, one of the leading reformers of the time, made a strong case for the achievements of modern science as they stood in 1927. Why should we focus on teaching the facts and principles of science?, he asked. "Because the citizen of our day uses modern science at each turn of his day's work." "If he is a thinking citizen," he went on, "he is ambitious to benefit by what he understands." In his view, science was the driving force in all of society, and "men need and desire a genuine interpretation of modern science as it appears in the home, street, and factory."[42]

Science had the practical power to improve every aspect of an individual's daily life, and science educators of this period pushed learning hard in this direction. Textbooks from the 1920s through the 1940s abounded with titles like *The Science of Everyday Life, Practical Physics, Chemistry at Work,* and *Biology and Human Affairs.*[43] All were written to provide students with facts and principles that could be applied to their immediate surroundings. Many science teachers today, in fact, make similar arguments about the value of knowing the facts learned in their science classrooms.

National Security

In the 1950s and 1960s, the utilitarian argument was made in terms of scientific "manpower" rather than personal utility. The development of the atomic bomb, radar, advances in quantum electrodynamics, and discoveries in countless other highly abstract specialized fields had created a different kind of "practical" need for science. World War II had revealed that the nation's survival no longer depended on whether a student knew how to adjust the damper on a coal furnace in the home or understood the basic ideas of personal hygiene. What mattered now—what increasingly seemed to be a matter of life and death—was how quickly scientists could advance the frontiers of knowledge, with the expectation that new discoveries could be turned to military advantage. Such knowledge was still practical, in the sense that it was used to "do things" in the world, but what might be done had little to do with the everyday matters of the individual. Instead, the purpose was to develop tools for national defense. Here the individual was replaced by the nation-state.

National security officials during these years were intensely interested in bolstering America's scientific and technical preparedness. President Truman set the country on a path toward massive remilitarization in the immediate postwar years as a means of countering the Soviet Union during the early days of the Cold War. The goal was technological supremacy, particularly in the area of nuclear weapons, and this required trained personnel. The outbreak of the Korean conflict in 1950 along with the tapering off of the postwar GI college-enrollment "bulge" created acute shortages of scientists and engineers. The director of the National

Research Council's Office of Scientific Personnel reported in a special issue of *Scientific American* on the manpower shortage in 1951 that in the "present emergency," there is a pressing need for scientists "to increase our national power and productivity." And the assistant director of the Office of Defense Mobilization reminded readers that the crisis wasn't going to end anytime soon. "We are dealing with a long-term emergency," he explained, one that "may be with us for 10 to 20 years."[44]

Concerns over the production of scientists and engineers grew throughout the decade. Even with the end of the Korean War, the new administration under President Eisenhower continued to build nuclear weapon systems and other cutting-edge military technologies to maintain the nation's security. But the competition was growing. A top-secret CIA assessment of Soviet science education in 1953 concluded that the Russians were "training a body of scientists and engineers which is increasing in size and quality and approaching comparability with that of the United States." The report pointed specifically at the disparities at the high school level, where the Soviets appeared to be placing "far greater and more consistent emphasis on scientific subjects ... than is found in the United States." In response, the House committee overseeing the appropriations for the National Science Foundation recommended an increase in funding that was eight times its previous level, with the bulk of it to be used for new programs in science teaching.[45]

The burning focus on science education for national defense grew white-hot following the October 1957 Soviet launch of Sputnik. The insistent arguments for better science teaching that had until then been limited to the committee rooms in Washington now spilled over into living rooms, school board meetings, and the mainstream press. An article in *Business Week* explained what was at stake: "The reason for so much concentration on the education of scientists is clear enough. Military supremacy in this age of the H-bomb and the earth-girdling rockets may be won by the side with the largest supply of well trained and well utilized scientists." *Life* magazine published a more widely circulated "urgent" series of issues devoted to the crisis in education complete with unfavorable comparisons between easygoing American schools and their rigorous, science-focused Russian counterparts.[46] It wasn't long before Congress passed the $1 billion National Defense Education Act in 1958, which combined with a tripling of the budget for the National Science Foundation to provide funds for improving science education through new high school textbooks and curriculum materials, innovative film and other instructional media, better laboratory facilities and equipment, summer institutes to improve science teacher content knowledge, and fellowships for graduate study.[47]

Despite the convictions by some that the national-security education crisis would last for decades, it was surprisingly short-lived. While the Cold War continued through the 1980s, détente with the Soviets and a crushing economic recession in the 1970s resulted in a federal pullback of science research funding.[48] Personnel surpluses and unemployment, particularly in the physical sciences, became commonplace—which is where things remained until the end of the decade when economists, corporate leaders, and government officials looked to science and technology-fueled innovation as a way to jump-start the stagnant US economy.

Economic Growth

Calls to harness science education for the nation's economic growth were prominent for a time in the mid-nineteenth century before taking up a permanent place in our public discourse beginning in the 1970s. Arguments for the utilitarian benefits of science resonated strongly with school boards and administrators as well as civic leaders in the United States in that earlier period. As a country pursuing westward expansion, knowledge about agriculture and natural resources related to mineral deposits, timber, and water were highly prized, as was knowledge pertaining to new systems of transportation, communication, and manufacturing as the country entered a period of intense industrialization. To meet these needs, Congress passed the Morrill Land-Grant Act in 1862, which provided funds from the sale of federal land to support colleges and universities "in order to promote the liberal and practical education of the industrial classes." The focus on the practical was front and center. The establishment of such institutions, supporters insisted, would encourage the application of scientific knowledge to improve productivity and stimulate economic development across the nation. Universities in places such as Wisconsin, Minnesota, New York, and California, among numerous others, stepped in or were established to fulfill this mission.[49]

The justification for this investment in science was evident during the groundbreaking of the new University Building on the grounds of the recently established Illinois Industrial University (the land-grant school that would become the University of Illinois). Presiding over the ceremony, the state superintendent of public instruction told the assembled crowd that the primary purpose of the school was to "*utilize* education in the interest of productive industry, to *deploy* the shining battalions of science out upon the open plains of life, and bring them to support the ubiquitous and gigantic activities of the age." This was, he insisted, a new age of education that would give the toiling masses the knowledge to "lay the iron rails, stretch the telegraphic wire," knowledge that would "let the anvils ring, the forges blaze, the shuttles fly, [and] the spindles hum." In their science classes, students would "peer into the mysteries of soils, of animal and vegetable life and growth, bend upon them the apocalyptic light of the solar ray, clap on them the vise and thumb-screw of chemical analysis, and wrench and torture their secrets from them." These were undoubtedly grandiose claims, but such claims made the crucial point that taxpayer dollars would be well spent—a positive return on investment was assured.[50]

The economic argument was resurrected a century later in response to the era of stagflation, unemployment, and energy shocks of the 1970s. The nation seemed stuck in a rut and was being outcompeted on the international stage. The enemy this time was Japan, which had expanded its global market in consumer electronics and fuel-efficient automobiles at the expense of American manufacturing. In 1980, a National Science Foundation report called on science education once again to rise to this new challenge. "During the coming decades," the authors wrote, "we are likely to be confronted with increasing competition, both from already industrialized countries and from those newly emerging industrialized countries with enormous labor resources." It seemed obvious, to them at least, that the ability to compete will "depend increasingly on our ability as a Nation to strengthen our technological and scientific enterprise."[51]

The specific case for science education in this new era was decidedly less clear than it had been in the 1950s. During that postwar decade, mastery of fields such as advanced electronics, nuclear physics, and aeronautic engineering was vital in the race with the Soviet Union. In the late 1970s and 1980s, the arguments for advanced training didn't get much further than calls for increasing student numbers in the sciences, which were believed to be the foundation for new technologies on which innovations in manufacturing and industry would be based. It was taken on faith that such innovations would serve as the engine of American economic growth. But the causal relationship between "innovation" and economic growth was far from firmly established. As one newspaper report put it, "no one seems to know the exact economic benefit of pure research, but most scientists, and many economists, argue that the entire economic life of the nation could suffer [if science is neglected]."[52] What remained, despite the ambiguity, was an argument based on the utility of science content knowledge—the only difference was that the beneficiary was now the nation's economic health rather than its defense capabilities.

The science-education "crisis" machine fired up in the 1980s as a result, and the justifications landed squarely on the question of economic survival. Among the flurry of reports at this time, two of the more significant came out in 1983. The first and most prominent was *A Nation at Risk: The Imperative for Educational Reform*. It led off with the dire assessment that the country's "once unchallenged preeminence in commerce, industry, science, and technological innovation is being overtaken by competitors throughout the world." The "risk," it noted, wasn't just that Japan and South Korea were producing more cars or steel more efficiently; "it is also that these developments signify a redistribution of trained capability throughout the globe." A fundamental reassessment of the American educational system was desperately needed.[53]

While the report's focus was on excellence in education generally, it took little effort to see the strong emphasis on science and mathematics. Five months later, the National Science Board offered its own "urgent" message to the American public in its report *Educating Americans for the 21st Century*. Our schools, it said, were failing to prepare students for the future. "The world is changing fast," the board wrote. "Already the quality of our manufactured products, the viability of our trade, our leadership in research and development, and our standards of living are strongly challenged," and the solution was, of course, to provide students with "a firm grounding in mathematics, science, and technology."[54]

This economic utility argument has been at the top of the list of reasons we teach science ever since. Journalist Thomas Friedman ratcheted up the nation's economic anxiety most recently in 2005 with the publication of his book *The World is Flat*, in which he highlighted the danger that the rise of China and India pose to America's position in the new knowledge economy. In the digitally connected world, he explained, technical expertise can be easily tapped from anywhere, and the United States needed to bolster the science education of its workers to keep its edge.

Friedman's book (along with the ever-present economic concerns among government officials and policymakers) triggered a series of reports and policy documents that have continued to beat the economic-utility drum. The most notable of these was the National Academy of Sciences report released in the fall of 2005, ominously titled *Rising above the Gathering Storm*. Echoing

Freidman's book, the committee drafting the report warned that "a substantial portion of our workforce finds itself in direct competition for jobs with lower-wage workers around the globe . . . just a mouse-click away." And it was "deeply concerned that the scientific and technical building blocks of our economic leadership are eroding at a time when many other nations are gathering strength."[55]

Its top recommendation was more high-level science education. The committee specifically identified the need for scholarships to support ten thousand new science and math teachers and summer institutes for existing teachers to upgrade their content knowledge. It called for funds to train tens of thousands more Advanced Placement or International Baccalaureate science and mathematics teachers and more students to enter the advanced-training pipeline. Two years later, Congress took up the recommendations nearly unchanged and passed the America COMPETES Act in 2007, which President George W. Bush signed into law. The argument was apparently convincing.[56]

Other reports making the same case soon followed. The Carnegie Corporation of New York and the Institute for Advanced Study released *The Opportunity Equation* in 2009. The first words of the report's executive summary paint the familiar picture— "The United States must mobilize for excellence in mathematics and science . . . . The nation's capacity to innovate for economic growth and the ability of American workers to thrive in the global economy depend on a broad foundation of math and science learning." Catchwords like transformation, innovation, productivity, and growth are sprinkled liberally throughout the text, and the means to achieve these goals is clear—we need to reform schools in "ways that place math and science more squarely at the center of the educational enterprise."[57]

The Carnegie Corporation subsequently funded the development of the Next Generation Science Standards (NGSS) in 2010, a revision of the standards documents (such as those that came from Project 2061 and the National Science Education Standards) developed in the wake of the crisis of the 1980s that currently serve as the template for science education reform. In the section of the splash page of the NGSS website devoted to why we need new science standards, the first box makes it clear—"Economic innovation depends on a broad foundation of math and science learning."[58]

At this point in our nation's history, knowledge appears to be power indeed. Many believe mastery of science concepts, theories, and techniques is the means for industry to grow and for the country to prosper. In the cutting-edge capitalistic global society we live in, science-driven technological progress is the currency that makes it all go. Much has changed over the past one-hundred-and fifty-plus years without question. In the early days, it was argued that knowledge of the natural world would benefit "the lot of the countryman and of the workmen in towns" through improved agricultural practices or more efficient manufacturing. Between the wars, science was touted for its everyday utility in managing the affairs of the home or local community—better bedroom ventilation or town sanitation. A hard shift to the nation-state as the primary beneficiary came with World War II (though arguments for personal utility can still be found), and the competition between nations has continued with the international economic challenges topping the list. While the contexts and beneficiaries have changed, the argument across it all has been essentially the same—that understanding the facts of science allows us to *do things*, that such knowledge is useful in enabling us to get by and thrive in the world. And this is a powerful reason why we teach science in school.[59]

Science Education for Democracy

Although the *utilitarian* argument (particularly as it appeared after World War II with its focus initially on national security and, later, global economic competition) has been the one that's moved the policymaking and government-funding needle, rarely has it appeared alone in discussions about the benefits of science education. Since the middle of the twentieth century, it has almost always been paired with the *democracy* argument. In 1948, for instance, Morris Meister (the principal of the famed Bronx High School of Science) acknowledged the importance of "maintaining a full and steady flow of able scientists" after the war *and* for promoting science education "among the citizens of a democracy." Over sixty years later, not much had changed. In 2009, authors of *The Opportunity Equation* coupled calls for more technical training with talk of democratic goals. "The nation's capacity to innovate for economic growth and the ability of American workers to thrive in the global economy," they stated, "depend on a broad foundation of math and science learning"—adding, "as do our hopes for preserving a vibrant democracy."[60]

The two ideas often appear to be joined at the hip, the one—democracy—serving as the ennobling twin to its materialistic workforce-training sibling. Each promises something of value. The power of the utilitarian argument comes from seeing science education as the engine of economic prosperity and the key to national security. The strength of the democratic argument, in contrast, lies in its appeal to the higher virtues of self-governance, collective decision-making, and political equality. Democracy is one of those ideas like motherhood and apple pie that carries with it emotional weight. It appeals to our foundational belief in fairness, justice, and rationality even, sparking a little tingle in our civic souls. Who, after all, could possibly object to an education that promotes democratic ideals?

Although most everyone has an instinctive, generally favorable disposition toward anything that bolsters civic participation, the democratic argument for science education is harder to characterize than the cultural, better-thinking, or utilitarian arguments. The term itself, "democratic," is inherently slippery in its vagueness. Does it refer to a system of government or an ideal of equality? A notion of fairness? A commitment to freedom? Another definitional challenge comes from the fact that the democratic argument relies in places on elements of the other three arguments— rational thinking (part of the better-thinking argument), for example, is often deemed key to democratic decision-making. A third challenge comes from the fact that the idea of science education for democracy itself has changed over the years. It began its life as a counterweight to the elitism of classical college preparatory studies and narrow disciplinary training, then switched to a means of dealing with a rising expert class during the 1950s and 1960s, and most recently became a way to promote general civic engagement.[61]

That said, given its distinctive place in the public mind and its longstanding presence in arguments for the importance of science education in the United States (it's a goal educators have repeatedly voiced since at least the 1930s), it seems worth exploring just what the democratic argument has entailed over the past hundred years and what we currently mean when we invoke it to determine whether it really is something worth pursuing in schools.

Some of the first references to science education and democracy came in the late 1910s, and they had little to do with citizen participation in democratic processes. Right around then, a rising professional education establishment called for a radical reorientation of school science teaching. In the decades prior, only a fraction of the school-age population attended high school (3.3 percent in 1900) and, even though most of those who did attend had no plans to go on to college, the high school science curriculum was nevertheless set mainly by the colleges and universities. High school enrollments exploded over the next few decades, shooting up over 400 percent from 1900 to 1920 and nearly doubling again from 1920 to 1930.[62] It seemed clear to the educational leaders of the time that a science program organized around traditional disciplinary knowledge was a poor fit for these new students. The needs of the children of farmers, tradespeople, and unskilled laborers, they felt, were not being met, and any attempt to foist on them a college-preparatory education was viewed as, in a word, undemocratic.

In 1918 a committee of the National Education Association issued a landmark report making a case for the reorganization of the curriculum. In that document, *The Cardinal Principles of Secondary Education*, the authors recognized that "the character of the secondary-school population has been modified by the entrance of large numbers of pupils of widely varying capacities, aptitudes, social heredity, and destinies in life." Moreover, given their commitment to an ideal of democracy that, for them, meant that education should be designed for all, they argued for shifting the focus away from the established school subjects and disciplines and toward the everyday needs and interests of the students—things such as personal health, worthy home membership, civic participation, and jobs. Education in a democracy, they wrote, "should develop in each individual the knowledge, interests, ideals, habits, and powers whereby he will find his place and use that place to shape both himself and society toward ever nobler ends."[63]

The changes were especially notable for the science curriculum. In the years leading up to the *Cardinal Principles Report*, scientific work in the United States had become increasingly specialized and abstract, having gotten to the point where the average person struggled to see its relevance, much less possess any basic understanding of it. School science increasingly mirrored this state of affairs. In the follow-up report from the science subcommittee, the members expressed concern about the proliferation of specialized courses and the lack of coherence from one to the next. They wrote that "science for high school students" had been mainly organized "for the purpose of giving information and training in each of the sciences," that the material covered was dictated by the logic of the disciplines. In the spirit of democracy, "steps should be taken . . . to prevent this increase in number and in specialization from diminishing the value of the instruction from the standpoint of the general needs of pupils and the needs of society" (clear elements of personal utility here). A "democratic" education, in this formulation, was viewed as one that met the needs of all students rather than just a select elite.[64]

By the 1930s, talk about democracy and education increasingly was tied to ideas about the harmonious operation of community life. "Life enrichment through participation in a democratic social order," educators believed, should be the primary goal of education—though what that meant precisely wasn't completely obvious. Much of it had to do with the simultaneous satisfaction of the individual's personal needs and the larger needs of society, which were many as the country fell into deeper economic depression. "Functional learning"—a forerunner of scientific literacy—was a key phrase of the time, defined as learning that enabled students to use knowledge of the content, process, and attitude of science in the practical situations of life. It was hoped that life enrichment through science education would contribute to the progress of society to the ultimate benefit of everyone.[65]

The nation's faith in democratic principles came in for harsh scrutiny in the years leading up to World War II. Public concerns about the rise of communism in the Soviet Union following the revolution of 1917 intensified with the establishment of brutal dictatorships across Europe in the twenties and thirties. By the late 1930s, the specter of totalitarianism in all forms (fascist or communist) along with the economic and social chaos of the worldwide depression prompted serious questions about the viability of democratic systems of government. Some critics laid the blame at the feet of the ever-expanding scientific worldview. They argued that the widespread acceptance of science in all facets of human life (particularly as it crept into fields like psychology, sociology, and ethics) contributed to a cultural relativism that would inevitably erode democratic ideals and result in a slide into authoritarianism.[66]

With the world on the brink of war, though, leading philosophers and public intellectuals pushed back against this characterization. Far from undermining democracy, they argued that science was closely aligned with it. Just as public policies were tested in practice following a process of legislative deliberation and enactment, so too did science proceed using an experimental method in which theories rose or fell depending on how they played out in the natural course of events. Supporters argued that science and democracy both embodied ideals of fairmindedness, deference to empirical evidence, and commitment to consensus. The sociologist of science Robert Merton famously offered a robust defense of science and democracy when he articulated his version of the scientific "ethos"—an ethos that was aligned with those of democratic, open societies (and antithetical to totalitarian political systems). Merton's contribution, written explicitly in response to the rise of Nazism, was part of a raft of anti-fascist works from intellectuals during this period in which science and democracy were seen as cut from the same cloth.[67]

Educational leaders of the time repeatedly engaged in discussions equating science and democracy. This was no doubt due to the influence of the philosopher and educator John Dewey. For decades, he advocated for education that would contribute to democratic forms of collective living, the virtues of which in the best instances were those of science. In July 1939, the science educator and National Education Association president Reuben Shaw gave a nationally broadcast radio address building on these ideas, making a case for science education as a means of strengthening the nation's democratic system of government. "There is a close relationship between the progress of science, and of education and of democracy, and of civilization," he declared, and that progress "comes in just about that order." Science, he explained, tests all of our knowledge, discarding what doesn't hold up. Education takes the knowledge deemed true and disseminates it to the people. "Democracy then goes still farther," he added, "and endeavors to translate those facts and viewpoints into human relationships that will be accepted by the majority." The process of science and the process of democracy were, he insisted, nearly identical. The more the public understood the basic methods of science, the stronger American democracy would be.[68]

Other claims about the value of science education for democracy at the time rested less on the equivalence between science and democracy and more on the ability of science to develop critical-thinking skills to be used in the course of democratic deliberation. In the 1942 *Science Teaching for Better Living* report from the National Committee on Science Teaching, the authors highlighted how important such thinking was. "Scientific method or critical thinking is especially important in a democracy such as ours," the authors wrote, "where every person has a voice in public affairs." "The hope of democracy lies in the ability of citizens to study pertinent problems and arrive at safe conclusions." Here the payoff for learning the scientific method came in its application outside of science to solve social problems. Mastery of technical, science content knowledge had little relevance in this view of science for democracy. It was the mastery of scientific thinking skills that was seen as far more important.[69]

This changed after the war. During the years following the Allied victory, suddenly the most pressing social problems of the day seemed directly related to the effects of science and technology—the control of atomic weapons, the development of atomic energy, the dangers of radiation from nuclear fallout, the preservation of the water supply, and the like. The social and political problems of this era seemed to require a deep understanding of technical knowledge far beyond the average citizen's capacity. How could decisions about science-related public policy be made if the public making the decisions didn't know the underlying science?

The solution, at least for some, lay in a new way to think about the primary goal of science education. It seemed to be a given that world affairs were increasingly dependent on specialized scientific knowledge and that this dependence was only going to increase over time. It was also clear that the average citizen in a democracy—the citizen who was ultimately responsible for making various policy decisions in this ever more scientific world—was never going to master the specialized knowledge needed in all areas of public concern. The aim couldn't be to teach more disciplinary content knowledge, an impossible task to be sure. But neither could it be to strip away the facts and theories of science and only attend to the process—the scientific method in some general, problem-solving sense—as some had advocated in the years before the war.

What was needed was a science education that helped students understand what science was and how it worked, that it was a specialized enterprise that operated through the integration of process and content knowledge. It was an activity pursued by small communities of researchers—experts in the field. Science education for democracy, in this view, aimed at learning *about* science and who did science so that one could recognize who possessed the necessary expertise concerning a given science-related social problem.

This approach was central to the new science courses and programs developed as part of the college general-education movement of the 1940s and 1950s. As returning veterans enrolled in American colleges and universities on the GI Bill after the war, campus leaders struggled with what sort of education would best prepare them for the postwar world. The problem of general versus specialized—that is, technical or vocational—education was front and center, especially during this era of increasing specialization and concerns about overall social cohesion. Educational leaders at several campuses (places like the University of Chicago and Columbia) had jumped into the general-education arena. The center of the movement in science, though, was at Harvard University, where James Conant spearheaded efforts to develop the new science courses that would best prepare students for their roles as citizens in the science-infused postwar world.

In the landmark 1945 Harvard report, *General Education in a Free Society* (the well-known Redbook), the committee charged by Conant explained their approach to the problem of expertise. "Since no one can become an expert in all fields, everyone is compelled to trust the judgment of other people pretty thoroughly in most areas of activity." The educational need, therefore, was for a level of knowledge and understanding that would enable someone "to distinguish the expert from the quack, and the better from the worse expert." "From this point of view," the report explained, "the aim of general education may be defined as that providing the broad critical sense by which to recognize competence in any field."[70]

The concern with how best to deal with expertise in the American political system persisted through the 1960s as science-related social challenges piled up. The Cold War was intensifying, and there were new worries over environmental degradation and overpopulation. The launch of Sputnik brought the educational challenge into sharp focus, and in 1959 a report from President Eisenhower's Science Advisory Committee (PSAC), *Education for the Age of Science*, put forward perhaps the most cogent science-education-for-democracy argument of the postwar period. The authors stated that the increasing reliance on expert knowledge made it imperative for a democratic society to have "millions of well-educated citizens who can comprehend what the specialists and the leaders are proposing, and who have a chance to judge these proposals wisely." The ability to judge, however, would come not from the public understanding the science content itself but rather from understanding how science generally operated, which expertise to rely on, and what the larger scientific enterprise required from society for its further advance.[71]

It was in this period that the postwar form of the *cultural* argument came into play as a means of realizing the larger democratic goal of science education. As explained in the PSAC report, the goal for the student was to "gain insight into the methods and concepts of science so that he can understand the world of science in which he lives." That "world of science" included recognizing and appreciating the scientific habits of mind, the communal nature of the research enterprise, the commitment to the disinterested pursuit of truth, and the unique role of expertise in the modern world—a role that by its very nature required public resources and, at the same time, insulation from careless public interference. As so many believed at the time, "a national effort is required to strengthen our scientific and technological efforts in all fields," but "in a democracy such an effort can succeed only if it has widespread public understanding and support."[72]

For many scientists then, ensuring the success of science within the context of the country's democratic political system was seen as crucial, and it was no easy problem to solve. The geneticist Bentley Glass insisted that "a populace uncomprehending, superstitious, and resistant to the novel ideas of the scientist" would be the country's downfall. "Somehow, and soon, mankind must become truly scientific in spirit and endeavor," he wrote. "Otherwise we face oligarchy, and eventual collapse of our form of civilization, our way of life."[73] This was serious business indeed.

Since the "age-of-science" years of the fifties and sixties, the sophistication of the science-education-for-democracy argument has gone down more than a few notches. In recent decades the reasoning behind it has increasingly relied more on a straightforward content-mastery mindset. Perhaps this is partly the result of the growing concerns over student performance on national and international tests (that inevitably measure student ability to recall the assorted facts of science), which coincided with the ascendence of the economic-growth justification for teaching science that got rolling in the late 1970s.

The physicist James Trefil has been the most prominent advocate for this approach, representing the science branch of the cultural-literacy movement that gained prominence in the late 1980s with the efforts of E. D. Hirsch. In his 2008 book *Why Science?*, Trefil offers what he calls the "argument from civics"—his version of the democratic argument. He begins with a working definition of democracy, which amounts to people having a say in policy decisions affecting their lives. And given that, as he sees it, "a good portion of the political debate in this country is going to be generated by advances in scientific and technological fields that are just coming over the horizon" (he cites the use of stem cells and therapeutic cloning as examples), he argues that the public needs to know enough of the relevant science to be able to participate in those policy deliberations, or, as he puts it, to "enter the debate." Those unfamiliar with the basic science of stem cells or cloning (to build on his examples) would be excluded from the discussion. They simply would not be able to make their "voices be heard."[74]

This argument has nothing to do with understanding the process of science or the culture of the scientific community; it's only about having some minimal amount of content knowledge so as to be familiar with what people are talking about, nothing more. And Trefil stresses the "minimal" in his explanation. The prescription for science teaching that issues from this form of the argument is basically to teach a lot of scientific facts so that when citizens encounter science-related policy issues in the news, they more or less know what they are about. Ironically, Trefil goes on to say that once someone does get "into the debate," they can quickly move on to engage the real issues at hand, issues that he points out rarely have to do with the science itself.

Another version of the democratic argument that's popped up since the turn of the most recent century similarly prioritizes content knowledge, but with an added dash of understanding of the scientific process or method. The 2007 National Research Council Report *Taking Science to School*, for example, states that students should be proficient in, among other things, the ability to "generate and evaluate scientific evidence and explanations." This skill is vital because "a democracy demands that its citizens make personal and community decisions about issues in which scientific information plays a fundamental role." Therefore, citizens "need a knowledge of science as well as an understanding of scientific methodology" in order to intelligently make those decisions.[75]

This argument suggests that the average citizen in possession of this knowledge would not only know what is being talked about in the news or social media (the Trefil standard) but also be able to critically evaluate the scientific claims being made with respect to the issue in question. The assumption here (though it's never clearly specified) is that a proper science education would enable someone to *independently* assess the validity or relevance of the science they encounter in the public sphere. While this makes good copy, it is not close to being realistic. If scientists themselves don't feel capable of evaluating the credibility of research outside their specialized fields, how possibly could the average citizen evaluate such work?[76]

Since the early decades of the twentieth century, we've had a range of somewhat distinct democracy-focused arguments for science education in the United States. There was the egalitarian, science-education-for-all version that emerged in the 1920s as schooling dramatically expanded to include those from all walks of life rather than just the college-bound upper middle class, with the result being a shift in curricular emphasis away from disciplinary knowledge taught for its own sake toward practical knowledge for daily life. Following this was a conception of science and democracy as mutually reinforcing social systems in the middle decades of the century (mainly in response to the rise of totalitarianism overseas). Most recently, at least since the 1950s, the democratic argument has been concerned primarily with how the public might best discharge its civic duty—the expectation that citizens participate in decision-making through the democratic political process—faced with what seems to be a growing number of science-related social issues.

Advocates for science education in this most recent era have variously emphasized cultural approaches (understanding and appreciating the role of scientists as experts), the better-thinking approach (highlighting the importance of critical thinking skills as a key element of political deliberation), and a content approach (knowing enough of the basic science to gain entry to the debate). All would likely agree with the version of the democratic goal as stated in the 1996 National Science Education Standards—to "educate students who are able to . . . engage intelligently in public discourse and debate about matters of scientific and technological concern." Who would disagree with that? The trick is to dig beneath the pretty sentiment to see what specific kind of science education such engagement would actually require.[77]

* * *

Looking across the range of justifications put forward over the past one-hundred-and-sixty-plus years, what becomes immediately apparent is that not all of these arguments carry the same weight today. Science education for utility would come in at the top of a present-day ranking—specifically utility related to national concerns about economic growth. The repeated references to this goal in recent education policy documents along with the hundreds of millions of dollars of federal funding devoted to increasing the number of students going into the STEM (science, technology, engineering, and mathematics) pipeline—

especially during periodic times of crisis—seem more than suffi-
cient to put this one in the first spot. In the second tier, I would put
science education for democracy (based on its frequency of mentions), better thinking (the critical-thinking argument and general
commitment to rational thought—a goal commonly voiced by
advocates), personal utility, and culture (science is an extraordinary human achievement that most scientists and educators
acknowledge).

All these arguments for teaching science (in tiers 1 and 2) are
evident in most of the recent statements about the importance of
science education made by panels of experts, scientists, teachers,
science-education researchers, and government officials. While
some might be emphasized more than others in any given document, all these justifications have currency in discussions about
why we teach science and therefore should be on the docket for
examination.

The arguments that we can safely set aside include the out-
dated belief that science education exercises the mind, resulting
in greater mental discipline. Any version of this argument updated
for the present would fall into the current critical-thinking/rational-
thought version of the better-thinking argument already included
in tier 2 above. We can dispense with the moral-uplift argument
as well, which enjoyed its time in the sun only in the last decades
of the nineteenth century. While there may be some science-
education advocates today who would still line up behind this
sort of justification, it's not found in formal policy documents
today or even in those of the past seventy years or so.

The two tiers of justifications break down fairly cleanly into
what many have long considered the two larger purposes of science education that I mentioned at the outset: (1) teaching science

to produce future scientists, what I call the *technical-training* goal; and (2) teaching science for the non-scientist (or layperson), which many have referred to as *science for general education*.

Tier 1	Science education for national utility (economic growth, national security)	*Technical training*
Tier 2	Science education for democracy	*Science for general*
	Science education for better thinking	*education*
	Science education for personal utility	
	Science education for culture	

The technical-training goal has always been concerned with producing the personnel necessary to ensure that the United States maintains its technological edge in the realm of national security and so that US-based corporations and the nation maintain their edge in the global economy. Education for this goal typically entails mastery of disciplinary content knowledge; facility with measurement, experimentation, and analysis; skill in calculation and the solving of typical textbook problems; and the ability to engage in the relevant scientific practices. This goal, in other words, begins and ends with the internal workings of science. All the arguments for science education in tier 2, in contrast, are arguments for why someone who has no plans to enter a science-related technical field should nonetheless still learn science—that is, this is science education for the citizen.

In the chapters that follow, we'll look at how well the technical-training goal maps onto the larger purposes of high school education in America and whether the high school science program is best positioned to accomplish the "fill-the-science-pipeline" agenda that many advocates call for. We'll then consider the remaining tier 2 goals of science education, those that fall within the science-for-general-education side of things, to see how those might fare in terms of likelihood of achievement within the current system. However, before diving into all that, we need to take stock of where things currently stand in American science classrooms and ask whether science education, even in ideal circumstances, can accomplish any of the goals many claim that it should.

PART 2
WHAT WE DO

CHAPTER 2

THE SCIENCE EDUCATION
WE HAVE

There has always been an odd disconnect between what we say science education offers us and what we actually teach in science classrooms. On the one hand, advocates are quick to point out all the presumed benefits we've read about in the opening chapter—the thinking skills, personal utility, contributions to economic innovation, and so on—for why science education is so important to the general public. Yet when it comes to putting together the textbooks, lessons, and experiences for students in those classrooms, teachers, policymakers, textbook writers, and the rest seem to jump—almost without thought—to mastery of disciplinary content knowledge as the immediate educational objective with a side of doing science here and there. In some ways, this isn't surprising. The facts, concepts, and theories about the world that scientists have produced over the years are, for many, just what science is. It is this content knowledge that enables us to brilliantly make sense of so much we see around us and provides the foundation for all the marvelous technologies that make our lives safer, healthier, more productive, and more interesting. Why wouldn't that be the focus?

But a fuzzy logic connects all the presumed benefits of learning science with the classroom emphasis on facts, concepts, and theories. And this logic—that bridges the yawning gap between the presumed benefits of studying science and how science is studied—is deceptively simple. It's based on a set of intuitively appealing assumptions that have guided science teaching for well over a century. If you hope to enter a science-related profession, according to this logic, then you naturally need to know the content of the assorted scientific disciplines. If you're weighing your options about some science-related social issue, it seems to make sense that it would help to understand the science behind it. If you want to think intelligently about everyday matters, well, what could be better than following the process scientists use?—the most logical and objective process there is. Combine all this with the increased policy emphasis on accountability and standardized assessments in schools, and you have a recipe for science teaching that leans heavily on disciplinary mastery, with five parts content and one part process.

That recipe is what passes these days—indeed in most any era—as "good" science education. It's what many believe will generate all of the benefits advocates have touted along the way, a "one-size-fits-all-goals" teaching approach. If we can only get students to *really learn* the content, solve all the textbook problems, and add in some solid hands-on work in the laboratory, then all the pie-in-the-sky elements of scientific literacy will be realized. (Sometimes even less thought goes into it than this; for a lot of people, science education just means teaching the facts, as simple as that.) The result is a science-education program that, on its face, seems to make a lot of sense—a program that any community would be proud to have. But when we look at the evidence, it turns out that such a program not only fails to produce the scientific literacy it aims for but also likely does more societal harm than good.

Of course, not all science teaching follows this disciplinary content-focused template. There are other innovative approaches to science teaching designed to accomplish more carefully articulated goals. I've described some of these in Chapter 1, where I laid out the range of arguments for science education in some detail. There are boutique research-practice partnerships where wonderfully complex kinds of science learning are happening every day too. But, as most of us know, these sorts of educational endeavors are not typical in American schools. When the goals are less well articulated and when the public accepts the common assumptions about how science education works, the result is the content-focused approach. The evidence for this is plain to see in the schools all around us. The science teaching that everyone settles on when local tax dollars are spent and schoolboard members' and parents' expectations actively shape the school curriculum is science teaching focused on disciplinary mastery.

"Is this really the case?" you might ask. Well, if you polled parents in the university town where I live about what they would like to see in the science-education program at the high school their children attend, there would be no shortage of opinions. You likely would hear comments about Advanced-Placement (AP) course offerings, college readiness, or how a good school should prepare students to do well on their ACTs or SATs. Such comments would align well with some of the newer online school—or neighborhood—ranking websites that use student test scores, college attendance, and AP course availability to gauge the quality of local schools. These tools point home buyers to the "best" places to live, and they rely on the general education metrics that most middle- to upper-middle-class parents and communities focus on. Suppose those same parents and community leaders ventured to comment on the science curriculum more specifically. In that case, they might talk about opportunities for students to do "hands-on" work, engage in authentic scientific inquiry, or learn new cutting-edge technologies—the more research-like the better.[1]

None of these responses would be surprising. They reflect the predominance of the technical-training goal that has overshadowed all the others and the current societal emphasis on test performance that parents see in the media time and again. The refrain is all too familiar. Science is where all the good jobs are! We need more scientists and engineers! Being scientifically literate means knowing a lot of scientific facts! (And maybe being able to do some science too.) It's no secret that people reflect what they hear in the news and online. These goals have thoroughly permeated our cultural landscape.

But rather than take my hypothetical neighbors' comments as hard evidence, we might consider some more concrete examples. Part of my responsibilities as a faculty member at my university is to teach an introductory science-teaching-methods course for students on the path to getting licensed as middle and high school science teachers. This course is offered at the beginning of their program in the fall semester after they've taken all the required university science content coursework. Students enter the program having already completed undergraduate science majors, and so their views of science are largely set.

One of the first activities I have them do is to imagine working in a school district where budget constraints have forced their high school to cut back all the science courses to one semester rather than the usual full year. The students get in groups by subject matter (biology, chemistry, physics, etc.), and I ask them to develop a course outline that will cover the essential material high school students should know in the eighteen weeks (one semester) they're allowed. I tell them, "Imagine this is the only exposure to this subject these students are likely to ever have—what is it that should be taught?" The challenge, of course, is to see what they believe the bare essentials of their subject are, the basics every citizen needs to know.

With no further guidance, the students huddle together and assemble their course outlines, which they write up on the large whiteboards in class. Each group gets the opportunity to describe just how they would use the limited time they have. Almost without fail, each and every group, year after year, shares what looks very much like a science textbook table of contents. In the most recent class, one biology group started off with a look at atoms and molecules. It then moved on to water and its properties and then covered plant and animal cells and their organelles, followed by cell division, genetics, tissues and organs, human organ systems (circulatory, respiratory, digestive, lymphatic, skeletal, nervous), evolution, and classification. They devoted about a week to each topic. The chemistry group began with energy and metric units of measurement and then moved on to the periodic table, models of the atom, balancing chemical equations (stoichiometry), thermodynamics, gas laws, and phase change. Physics groups put together a similar list of disciplinary topics covering everything from displacement, velocity, and acceleration, to the concept of force and Newton's laws of motion, to momentum, electricity and magnetism, and all the other greatest hits of physics.

When I asked the students why they included what they did on their course outlines (why they listed things as specific as "Gibb's free energy," "endoplasmic reticulum," and the "Kreb's cycle" as essential learning for high school students), they responded with statements like, "Because it's what we learned in high school," "We wanted to touch on everything so that it would prepare them for college," "Tradition," "We just wanted to hit them with as much information as possible in the limited time we had," and "It's important for daily life." When I asked the class how many of them could explain the Kreb's cycle or Gibb's free energy on the spot (given that, according to the groups, these are things *every* high schooler should know!), few were willing to step up with clear definitions or explanations. Instead, there were plenty of sideways glances and nervous laughter—this from individuals with undergraduate degrees in the sciences.

Clearly, these soon-to-be teachers, like so many before them, are operating with a view of science education defined by science-textbook content knowledge. When they think of what it means to teach biology or chemistry or physics or what have you, they default to lists of facts, concepts, and theories that they themselves learned initially in high school and then revisited in college in greater depth. Although on occasion they insist that the content should be useful in everyday life, more often than not, they see the learning of that content as necessary primarily because they think that their students will need to know it for some standardized test or because they'll encounter the concept again in college or that it might spark some interest and lead students to a science-related career. In other words, they default to the widespread assumption that most students *should* be on a college-prep pathway and that a good number of them will flow into the technical-training pipeline and fill all those science-related jobs waiting on the other end. It's an economic-utility mindset through and through, one shared by parents, business leaders, and policymakers as well.

One last illustration of this point is grounded firmly in the school science program of a suburban town of about 13,000 people roughly fifteen minutes from where I live, where they just built a new state-of-the-art high school. Although members of the community work in a range of occupations, a majority have at least a bachelor's degree, make their living in professional and technical fields, and enjoy above-average household incomes. The school is a gorgeous facility that cost somewhere around $190 million and required passage of a local referendum to finance it. It has a stunning interior atrium, classrooms with flexible seating to promote student interaction, floor-to-ceiling windows, a high-tech performing-arts center, expansive athletic fields, and the latest science laboratory apparatus and equipment.

Looking at the school's academic course guide, the first thing you see when you get to the science program is a page listing three levels of courses. The first level consists of the one course required of all ninth-graders—biology. At the next level, students have various options, including applied chemistry, chemistry, physical science, general physics, earth science, environmental science, scientific thinking, biotechnology, and advanced biotechnology. The top level consists almost entirely of AP courses (physics, environmental science, chemistry, and biology). In addition to these science offerings, the school has a separate program called Project Lead the Way, a national curriculum focused on preparing students for technical careers.[2] There are Project-Lead-the-Way tracks in engineering (with courses in engineering design, principles of engineering, and design and development) and biomedical science (with courses that cover topics such as the human body system, medical interventions, and biomedical innovations).

To help with long-range planning, the school has arranged the various options into sample course sequences that lead students down four potential "career pathways." The first three are "agriculture, food, and natural resources" (which lists jobs such as dietician, forester, and park naturalist); "health science" (dental hygienist, doctor, dentist); and "STEM" (astronomer, engineer, chemist). The fourth is labeled simply "non-science majors" and is just tacked on at the end (even though this is where most of the students will actually end up).

If you navigate to the science department's welcome page on the school website, you'll find its "mission statement." It includes references to technology, hands-on learning, and the students using their imagination to understand the natural world. At this level of generality, all the usual goals of science education are spelled out for curious parents and students—developing critical-thinking skills, problem solving, understanding how science applies to everyday life, becoming active members of an ever-changing society, and so on.

The details of the course guide, though, tell a different story— one about future careers, technical skills, college preparation, and AP coursework. Scientific literacy or any of the science-for-citizen goals are the last things that would occur to a parent or student reading through these course options. Even general science—a course historically designed to prepare students to understand science in their daily lives and think logically—is gone from this curriculum. The only thing resembling general science is the elective course "Scientific Thinking," which draws a total of only about thirty to forty students each year (out of a total school enrollment of over 1,500) and is unlikely to attract many of the top students who are moving along the various science-career, college-bound tracks. Those students need all the slots they can get for the AP courses they will undoubtedly top up their schedules with.

The disconnect between the goals stated in the science department's mission statement and the substance of the courses students take is striking. This is what you get when you let the default assumptions about good science education steer the curriculum— a content-focused program oriented toward technical training, workforce development, and college preparation. This outcome isn't unique to this particular school, of course. It's what you find when you survey science programs in schools across the country, especially those in the more affluent communities. This is the kind of science curriculum that most parents, policymakers, and local business leaders would ask for. Indeed, it's what they *have* asked for and built for themselves.

Many of you might not see any real problem at this point. So what if students are taking courses in biotechnology or AP physics? So what if they're only learning the technical content of the various sciences? Courses like these are both relevant (career-wise) and rigorous! Why can't they help students develop everyday problem-solving or critical-thinking skills too? And don't students need to understand basic (or more than basic) science if they hope to participate in conversations around science-related social issues? This is the argument many science education advocates make—that a "good," properly designed curriculum can accomplish *all of the goals* in question, that we don't need to pick and choose among them. This is what we get when we subscribe to the fuzzy thinking that connects what we say science education can accomplish with what actually goes on in classrooms. The reality, however, is that while we *hope* that all those science-for-general-education goals might be realized, what really seems to matter is that students get the technical training (content preparation) they need for the economic-growth utilitarian goal. And when you think about it, this shouldn't be at all surprising.

Take the science-education program from the high-achieving suburban community described above. Apart from the science courses like earth science and biology (setting aside the "Scientific Thinking" course that few students take), most of the rest are either career focused (biotechnology, engineering) or AP (which is career focused in a college-prep sort of way). The emphasis in these courses is almost always on mastering technical content. Students are expected to learn the facts and principles of the subject and how to solve typical textbook problems. In a chemistry class, for instance, students are taught the parts of an atom—that clouds of electrons at different energy levels surround a nucleus made up of protons and neutrons. They are taught how to balance chemical equations (stoichiometry) and how to calculate the mass of products produced given specific amounts of reactants or the pH of a particular acid in solution. This is simply what science teaching in these classes looks like. These are the very course outlines the preservice teachers came up with when asked to define the essential content in the one-semester-science-course activity!

The content emphasis is even more pronounced in the AP courses, which are designed to prepare students to take the end-of-year AP exam—an exam that, if passed, has the potential to reduce the number of course credits a student might have to take in college (and that a parent might have to pay for).

Established by the College Board in the 1950s, the AP program has always focused on the goal of content mastery in an effort to meet national needs. Boosting American human capital was and continues to be the centerpiece of its mission. The program was designed originally to address the technical personnel shortages after World War II and was readily enlisted by President George W. Bush in 2007 to help bolster the country's global economic-growth agenda. Dramatically increasing the number of AP teachers and students in science and mathematics was a key element of the America COMPETES Act passed that year. In science and math, the legislation aimed to add over 70,000 AP-qualified teachers who would, it hoped, reach an additional 700,000 students not currently taking those advanced courses.[3]

Critics have argued repeatedly that AP courses "cover too much material and do so too quickly and superficially," that they offer little more than "a forced march through a preordained subject." Many see courses in the sciences, in particular, as "overwhelming students with facts to memorize." While the College Board has made some efforts of late to emphasize scientific inquiry and reasoning skills in their science course guidelines and exams, recent studies show that teachers still feel tied to the test and spend much of their class time in test-prep work rather than engaging students in the kind of instruction that would produce meaningful learning of anything other than traditional disciplinary content. A glance at the most current course frameworks put out by the AP program in each of the sciences shows lists of units almost identical to the science-textbook table of contents the science-teachers-in-training offered up in the first-day methods course activity.[4]

Whether in AP or regular science courses, the teaching of science content in American high schools has predominated. Vocabulary, facts, concepts, theories, and problem sets routinely win out over nearly everything else. When the process of science comes into the picture, it almost always arrives via a scripted set of steps that students follow in the laboratory that produce questionable learning outcomes at best. A National Research Council committee conducted the most thorough examination of school science laboratory work in 2006. The authors of that work, *America's Lab Report*, concluded that "most science students in U.S. high schools today participate in laboratory experiences that are isolated from the flow of classroom instruction," that they empha-size "procedures to be followed," and leave students "uncertain about what they are supposed to learn." When laboratory work is implemented in the context of state standards, the committee reported that those standards often "support attainment of only one of the many goals of laboratory experiences—mastery of subject matter."[5]

Nothing much has changed in the years since that report was published. In a penetrating study that came out in 2019, two edu-cation researchers, Jal Mehta and Sarah Fine, wrote about their efforts to find examples of the best high schools across the United States, hoping to use those schools to highlight teaching prac-tices that foster deep and meaningful learning among students. They looked at charter schools, private schools, magnet schools, no-excuses schools, International Baccalaureate schools, and tra-ditional high schools. They followed every lead to try and locate places where innovative, powerful learning was happening. In the end, they visited thirty schools, spent over 700 hours observ-ing what took place within them, and interviewed hundreds of students, parents, administrators, and community leaders.

What they discovered and described in their book, *In Search of Deeper Learning*, was deeply disappointing. In these schools—schools they selected based on their stellar reputations—they found that "most classrooms were spaces to sit passively and listen," that "most academic work instructed students to recall, or minimally apply, what they had been told." When Mehta and Fine asked students what they thought the point of any given lesson was, the most "common responses were 'I dunno—it's in the textbook,' and 'maybe it'll help me in college.'" The pattern was the same across all subject areas, science included. The focus from day one was on content learning, calculation, and scripted laboratory work in the service of content learning.[6]

This is the science education we currently have in most of our middle schools and high schools across the United States. The question that we need to ask given this state of affairs is "How well does this approach to science teaching—even if done well—match up with what we hope to accomplish for the majority of students in our science classrooms?" We'll start by considering the technical-training goal before moving on to the benefits and goals that fall into the science-for-general-education bucket.

CHAPTER 3

SHOULD WE BE TRAINING MORE SCIENTISTS? THE NUMBERS SAY NO

Conventional wisdom tells us we need more scientists and engineers in the United States. This is one of the key planks in the technical-training science education platform on which many influential decision-makers currently stand. The nation's economic prosperity depends on it, so this version of the utilitarian argument goes. Ask anyone in your social or professional network, and they will likely agree. There may or may not be a scientific personnel "crisis" at the moment, but most people would certainly not disagree with the idea that it would be great if more young people went into the sciences. After all, science drives innovation, and we need to keep ahead of China, of course (though not so much the Russians anymore). Science and technology are also where the "good jobs" are these days. Any high school graduate heading down that path in college or even tech school is sure to end up financially secure for the rest of their life.

The reason we believe this is relatively straightforward. Blueribbon panels, government agencies, and prominent business leaders since the days of the postwar manpower shortages have told us again and again and again that this is the case (as we saw in chapter 1). The letter of support for the Next Generation Science Standards signed by over sixty businesses (including heavyweights such as Merck, Exxon Mobil, and 3M) trots out the same argument. "As business leaders," they write, "we fully understand the cause and effect relationship that exists between talent and innovation. Put simply, the availability of a creative and highly skilled workforce across America's cities, regions and states stimulates innovation and results in economic prosperity." Simple, right?[1]

Given the importance of this technical-training goal, one would expect that science education geared toward this end would serve a fairly significant percentage of the high school population. Sure, a lot of students won't end up in technical degree programs or jobs, but a good many undoubtedly will, and with the continued focus on plugging all the leaks in the STEM pipeline, the number of students going into the sciences must be growing. So let's crunch the numbers and see what we get.

According to the most recent data from the National Center for Education Statistics (NCES), about 4 million ninth-graders enrolled in public high schools in the fall of 2020. If we add the approximately 375,000 private school ninth-graders that year to those in the public schools, we get a total ninth-grade enrollment of around 4.4 million.[2] We'll start with these students, whom we would expect to graduate from high school in the spring of 2024 as the baseline. We'll deal in percentages rather than raw numbers to make things simple. That is, this cohort of ninth-graders will be our 100 percent. All of these students will show up in their first-year science class as 14 or 15 year olds. They will most likely be taking biology, but some will be in a general or physical science course as well, depending on the school. I've represented this population in Figure 1.

Figure 1 Incoming class of ninth graders (each figure represents 1 percent of the total).

Now, we know that all of these students, unfortunately, won't graduate from high school. The average cohort graduation rate is around 85 percent.[3] This is the percentage of students who graduate with their class after four years of continuous study. However, we're interested in the final educational attainment of our initial group, including those who eventually graduate after some time away or earn a GED (a test-based certification of high school completion). According to the NCES, the percentage of all 25 to 29 year olds in 2020 who completed four years of high school or some high school equivalency program was 94.8 percent.[4] So there actually isn't that much attrition going from our hypothetical group of ninth graders to high school completion (even if it took some of the group a few additional years to get it done). This gives us Figure 2.

Figure 2 High school completers (or equivalent).

The various science-education policy documents typically talk a lot about increasing standards and rigor to get students "college ready," which is partly the reason for all those AP courses. So let's see how many of our ninth graders make it to a degree of some sort. From the same NCES data set, we can see that 50 percent of 25 to 29 year olds have earned an associate's degree or higher, and 39.2 percent end up with at least a bachelor's degree. So, half of all our incoming ninth graders will end up with a degree of some sort, with most earning at least a four-year degree. This is represented in Figure 3.

Having 50 percent of this group completing an associate's or bachelor's degree is a pretty impressive accomplishment given that in 2000 only 31 percent of all adults 25 years old and over met this mark.[5] But the question we're really interested in is "How

Figure 3 Associate's or bachelor's degree earners in any subject.

many high school students end up making it through the *science-training pipeline* with a degree?" The National Science Foundation has consistently kept track of science degrees earned since the early 1960s. However, its data are limited to majors in the sciences, mathematics, and computer sciences. Surely we would want to include other science-related majors, such as those in the health professions leading to careers in nursing, physical therapy, and dental hygiene, where knowledge about biology, physics, and chemistry is likely to be helpful. Data from the NCES give us that.[6] The numbers and percentages of associate's and bachelor's degrees earned in 2018–19 in each of the science and science-related categories are shown in Table 1.

Taking the weighted average of the two types of degrees (associate's and bachelor's) makes a total of 27.3 percent science or science-related degrees combined. Applying that to our group of degree completers gives us about 14 percent of our original group

Table 1: Associate's and Bachelor's Degrees Earned by Subject Area

Associate's Degrees (2018-19)		
All associate's degrees (any major)	1,036,662	100%
Total science/science-related assoc. degrees	240,961	**23.2%**
Breakdown by subject		
Agriculture and natural resources	8,196	0.8%
Biological and biomedical sciences	7,299	0.7%
Engineering	6,367	0.6%
Engineering technologies	25,977	2.5%
Health professions and related programs	182,565	17.6%
Physical sciences and science technologies	10,557	1.0%
Bachelor's degrees (2018–19)		
All bachelor's degrees (any major)	2,012,854	100%
Total science/science-related bachelor's degrees	590,459	**29.3%**
Breakdown by subject		
Agriculture and natural resources	40,458	2.0%
Biological and biomedical sciences	121,191	6.0%
Engineering	126,687	6.3%
Engineering technologies	19,620	1.0%
Health professions and related programs	251,355	12.5%
Physical sciences and science technologies	31,148	1.5%
Weighted average (associate's and bachelor's degrees)		**27.3%**

of ninth graders (Figure 4). As you can see, despite all the talk about getting students into the science-training pipeline, in the end—even including a range of science-related majors (such as nursing, agriculture, and so on) in addition to the more obvious

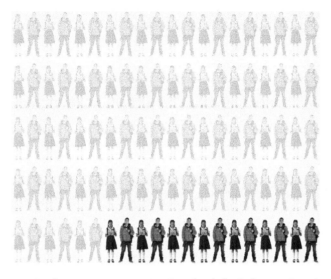

Figure 4 Students earning associate's or bachelor's degrees in science or science-related fields.

science majors that we're familiar with (for example, zoology, botany, chemistry, physics, geology, and atmospheric science)—about 86 percent of beginning high school students end up on the *outside* of that pipeline at one point or another. For the science pipeline boosters, this number has to be somewhat disappointing.

But there is one more bit of information to consider before we put the supply side of this accounting to bed—jobs. All of the students who end up earning degrees in the sciences, it turns out, don't always end up working in jobs or careers related to those degrees. Although somewhat dated now, a 2013 report from the U.S. Department of Commerce drawing on census data found that "the vast majority of workers who have been trained in science and engineering"—74 percent—"are not currently working in a STEM occupation."[7] The focus on STEM, of course, lumps together several degrees and occupations that fall outside of the natural sciences. It counts, for instance, degrees in computers, mathematics, statistics, psychology, and the social sciences as falling under the "STEM" label and does the same for occupations in those fields as well.

If we're looking at technical training in the natural sciences, however (the subject we're interested in this book), then we can omit these non-natural science STEM fields from the calculation. Doing this, limiting the field of degree in the Department of Commerce study (which looks just at bachelor's degrees) to the natural sciences (such as biological, agricultural, and environmental sciences; the physical sciences; and engineering and engineering-related fields) and comparing that to the reported fields of employment of those degree holders in science or science-related occupations (excluding computer work, mathematics, and the social sciences), we find that on average 54 percent of them are working outside of science/science-related occupations (which is not as low as the STEM field as a whole). On the flip side, though, this means that only 46 percent of those degree holders *are* working in science or science-related positions.[8] Applying that percentage to our initial group of ninth graders gives us a touch under 6.3 percent. But let's be generous and round up to 7 percent (Figure 5).

So as our group of average American ninth graders makes its way through high school to graduation (or some high school-graduation equivalent), moves on to college (or work), graduates from college (from either a two- or four-year institution), and enters the workforce. At the end of that line, only about 7 out of every 100 students will end up working in a science-related occupation. This means, naturally, that roughly 93 out of every

Figure 5 Student science-degree holders working in science or science-related occupations.

100 students will do things with their lives that don't require the professional use of science content or process knowledge. Given this, the takeaway question here is—How much technical training do high school students really need?

Some readers might counter this finding with a response along the lines of "Just because current educational attainment in science is lower than we'd like, it doesn't mean we shouldn't try and get the numbers up. We certainly can do better than this!" However, if history is any guide, it may very well be the case that we can't, at least not with our current political system and approaches to education reform. In 1972 a study conducted by two Harvard University researchers, Paul Doty and Dorothy Zinberg, found that between 1960 and 1970, the number of natural science college graduates (excluding engineering) was consistently just over 2 percent of the number of high school graduates in any given year. The "striking stability" of that number "during a period in which concentration in science was greatly encouraged," they wrote, "suggests that this is the optimal performance of the current educational system."[9]

If we look at a more extended timeframe and include the more comprehensive range of science degrees tracked by the National Science Foundation in its *Science and Engineering Indicators*, a biennial report designed to monitor the health of the American scientific enterprise, we find similar stability. Counting up bachelor's degrees across engineering and engineering technologies; agricultural and biological sciences; earth, atmospheric, and ocean sciences; and the physical sciences from 1964 to 2016, we find the total number of degrees fluctuates within a relatively narrow band of 13 to 17 percent of all bachelor's degrees with no noticeable overall trend either up or down. This is despite efforts by the NSF to increase those numbers, as can be seen in the peaks for education funding in the 1960s (the post-Sputnik era) and later during the standards/*Rising above the Gathering Storm* era beginning in the 1990s (Figure 6).[10]

"Now wait a minute," I can hear some readers say. "Maybe those numbers are right and only a small fraction of young people end up going through the science pipeline and ending up in science-related jobs. What about all the STEM jobs that are going unfilled? What about the huge demand for science-and-technology workers!?" We repeatedly hear that the twenty-first century is the century of the knowledge economy, that it's a STEM world out there, and that without funneling more students into the pipeline, we risk our country's future economic prosperity. Our global competitors will eat our lunch, so to speak.

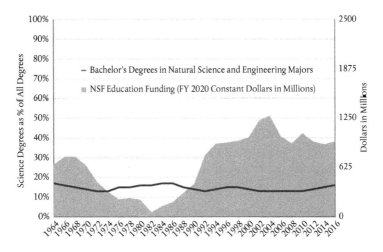

Figure 6 Bachelor's degrees in the natural sciences and engineering as a percentage of all bachelor's degrees awarded and NSF education funding in constant dollars.

Well, let's see what the jobs data tell us. Looking through the 2013 Department of Commerce report already mentioned, we find that the authors' tabulation of occupations using census data identified about 6 percent of the United States labor force as STEM workers. In addition to engineers, life scientists, physical scientists, secondary school science and math teachers, and science technicians, this number included social scientists and those in computer and mathematical occupations, workers we excluded from our calculations since their work isn't directly related to natural-science content knowledge. It also includes workers with and without degrees in the sciences, making this a generous estimate of the science-related workforce. And yet still—only 6 percent.[11]

Interestingly that same year, the Metropolitan Policy Program at the Brookings Institution released a report titled *The Hidden STEM Economy* that claimed traditional measures (like degrees earned) miss a significant number of technical or blue-collar jobs requiring STEM knowledge. Rather than focusing on job titles or college majors, the study authors instead asked workers to self-score the extent to which they relied on knowledge from six STEM domains in their daily work: biology, chemistry, physics, computers and electronics, and engineering and technology. They combined the ratings into a composite score for each occupation, which they ranked by the level of STEM knowledge required. Contrary to the familiar assumption that degreed professionals fill most STEM positions, the report concluded that "half of all STEM jobs are available to workers without a four-year college degree." When you add this to the other half (those jobs that do require a four-year degree), the total STEM workforce makes up 20 percent of all jobs in the United States.[12]

So what might be we take from this study? We might say that, hmm, 20 percent of all occupations in the United States currently (at least as of 2013) require high levels of STEM knowledge, and so it's a good thing for high school science courses to focus on the technical-training goal. However, 20 percent isn't all that much more than the 14 percent of students who end up with associate's or bachelor's degrees in science-related fields, and those numbers seem about right if half the jobs don't require a bachelor's degree. So any claims about huge numbers of STEM jobs going unfilled aren't well supported by the data. But this isn't quite right. In all likelihood, the Brookings' study overestimates the number of jobs requiring science-content knowledge that are really out there. Setting aside questions about the reliability of the self-reporting methodology (wouldn't respondents likely err on the side of classifying their jobs as more sciency than they in fact are?), there are some serious face-validity issues.

One of the ways the Brookings' study gets to that 20 percent number is by including a range of non-professional (blue-collar) jobs that respondents indicated required STEM knowledge. Some examples of these are automotive service technicians and mechanics, HVAC (heating, ventilation, and air conditioning) mechanics and installers, computer and office machinery repairers, building inspectors, elevator repairers, and electricians. While such work certainly involves machinery and technology and science-like objects and phenomena such as simple machines, compressed gases, and electricity (things that one typically learns about in high school science courses), it's unlikely that the school-science knowledge these workers learned in high school contributed much to their ability to perform the jobs in question.

The tasks required for these kinds of jobs are typically learned in specific technical courses or through on-the-job training or apprenticeships. One recent study that sought explicitly to probe the role high school science courses play in preparing students for those blue-collar jobs in the "hidden" STEM economy determined that they actually didn't play much of a role. The researchers found no evidence to support their hypothesis that "non-college bound youth who take advanced academic STEM courses and applied STEM courses in high school will be more likely to hold jobs in the STEM economy and earn higher wages."[13] Employers, in fact, often didn't even look at the job candidates' high school record at all.

Another factor that overestimates the number of science-related jobs in that study is the inclusion of computer and mathematical science positions in its total. These are STEM jobs, of course. However, technical training in the natural sciences—the typical high school courses of general science, biology, chemistry, and physics—has little if any relevance for that sort of work. If we separate these out and tally only the top three categories of high-STEM-knowledge jobs found in the Brookings' study (architecture and engineering; life, physical, and social science; and healthcare practitioner and technical)—even with the self-reporting (and the inclusion of the social sciences!)—the total comes in at a much lower 9 percent.[14]

Perhaps a less roundabout approach might be simply to look at the latest Bureau of Labor Statistics occupational data. As of September 2021, that office reports the current number of all STEM jobs to be 10.2 million, which is about 6.8 percent of all jobs in the United States. This closely aligns with the Department of Commerce number from 2013. As we repeatedly hear in the news and in various policy documents, those jobs are projected to increase rapidly in the coming years. Indeed the Bureau of Labor Statistics puts the increase at 10.5 percent between 2020 and 2030, an increase 36 percent greater than the projected increase of all jobs during that period. But, once again, if we remove the computer, mathematical, and social science occupations from the total, the remaining percentage of STEM jobs falls to less than 3 percent, with a projected ten-year increase of around 6.4 percent—less than the projected 7.7 percent increase for all jobs over that period.[15] When adjusted to exclude jobs unrelated to the natural sciences, the science-related jobs category doesn't seem to be poised for the rapid growth many assume.

Summarizing the various reports and data sources from 2013 to the present, we're looking at a realistic range of 3 to 9 percent for the total number of science-related jobs in the current economy. Interestingly enough, the mid-point of this range seems to match up pretty well with the percentage of high school students (7 percent) who end up in the science-related workforce from the educational-attainment side of the equation we started with.

It's much more likely, though, that the actual number of student science graduates in science-related jobs falls in the lower portion of that range because, as mentioned earlier, not all students with science degrees end up in science jobs. Various studies have looked at what is called "utilization of science education for work" and found that somewhere between only one-third and one-half of all science and engineering undergraduate degree holders end up in the science workforce. In other words, according to these studies, we routinely have an oversupply of technically trained workers for available positions. Regarding bachelor's degrees in STEM fields, one recent study concluded that "colleges historically produce between 40 to 100 percent more STEM graduates, depending on the field, than are hired into STEM occupations each year." The data strongly align with the in-depth analysis of the supply and demand of technical talent conducted by former Sloan Foundation vice-president Michael Teitelbaum. The leading finding of his 2014 book, *Falling Behind? Boom, Bust, and the Global Race for Scientific Talent*, was that "the alarms about widespread shortages of shortfalls in the number of U.S. scientists and engineers are quite inconsistent with nearly all the available evidence."[16]

At this point, some of you might want to object to the repeated exclusion of certain categories of jobs from what I'm counting as science-related occupations. Perhaps you're okay with getting rid of the social sciences (which are obviously unrelated to what one learns in high school biology, chemistry, and physics classes) but less willing to grant that there's absolutely no connection between high school science coursework and computers or computational thinking and mathematics. There's a good deal of mathematics in physics after all, right? However, the technical-training argument (the most recent form of the utilitarian argument—science education for national economic prosperity) assumes that it's the *knowledge* an individual gains about the workings of the natural world—the facts, concepts, theories, and methods of biology, chemistry, and physics that fill up all those textbook tables of contents—that are useful to businesses and industries for spurring innovation and technological advance. As the business leaders wrote in their NGSS letter of support, the hope is that the standards will provide students with "a *content-rich* science education that will prepare them for college and careers." There seems to be little disagreement about what it is students should learn.[17]

The benefits of science study that one might come away with in addition to that knowledge, such as the ability to think more analytically or critically or more effectively solve problems, fall into a separate argument for science education, that of *better thinking*—the argument that deals with the development of intellectual skills that are generalizable beyond the science-content domains. We'll deal with that later on when we look at *science for general education*.

* * *

Before we leave the topic of science content knowledge and economic growth, it's worth addressing the recurring issue of international science test-score comparisons. Periodically we see in the press alarming stories about how poorly American students are doing compared to their peers from other countries. "U.S. Students Show No Improvement in Math, Reading, Science on International Exam," read a 2019 headline from a *US News & World Report* article reporting on the disappointing performance of American 15 year olds on the PISA test,[18] Government officials and policymakers frequently express concerns about the consistently low performance of American students or how other advanced industrial nations are outpacing us, and their voices get amplified in news stories splashed across the media landscape. It's true that U.S. students consistently score well below students in other countries across a range of assessments (though some feel that the comparisons are unfair). The PISA results had U.S. students ranked sixteenth in science among the seventy-five countries that participated. In a similar test known as TIMSS (Trends in International Mathematics and Science Study), U.S. science scores in 2019 ranked eleventh out of forty-six total countries at the eighth grade level.[19] But what does this really mean?

On the NGSS website page devoted to the need for standards, you find a link to the "Lagging achievement of U.S. students"—which cites our low PISA ranking—just after a link about the "Reduction of the United States' competitive edge."[20] The juxtaposition of these headlines reinforces the frequently made argument that we need to get our science test scores up if we hope to meet the global economic challenges the country faces. One proponent of this argument is Eric Hanushek, a senior fellow at Stanford University's Hoover Institution. He claims unequivocally that "growth is tightly tied to the skills of a country's population," and that "international tests such as PISA and TIMSS do a good job at measuring these important labor-force skills."[21] This presumed connection—between student science knowledge (as measured by international assessments) and economic growth (often measured by a country's per capita gross domestic product [GDP])—lies at the heart of human-capital theory, the idea that increased levels of education make individuals more economically productive. It turns out, though, that there are serious questions about how tight that link is and whether the theory has any validity at all.

As far back as 2000, researchers found problems with the repeated claims about the causal link between science and mathematics education and economic growth. There were issues with incomplete data sets, modeling ambiguity, and inconsistent results. Since then, efforts to tamp down what some have called an "obsession" with this test-score/economic-growth link have multiplied.[22] A 2021 study by international educational researchers Jeremy Rappleye and Hikaru Komatsu surveyed a range of research on human-capital theory and completed additional analyses that once again debunked the connection, finding it "grounded on unreasonable assumptions." They went on to insist that "much of the new global policy regime centered on international learning assessments seems to be founded on dubious statistical claims passed off as an 'evidence base.'"[23]

Sophisticated statistical analyses aside, the fact that the top sixteen countries in terms of PISA science scores in 2015 all ranked below the United States according to per capita GDP in 2021 seems to say it all.[24] Based on this, it appears there must be other factors that contribute far more to economic success than student test performance in science.

***

So, to what extent should K–12 science education focus on the goal of technical training, that is, having students primarily learn the content of the various scientific disciplines? After running the numbers, it seems pretty obvious that this wouldn't be the most efficient use of our scarce educational resources.

Let's accept the claim that science and technology are essential to industrial innovation and economic growth in the twenty-first century. It may well be that this sort of research-and-development activity is indeed the driver of a nation's prosperity in the global knowledge economy. Whether this is truly the case isn't the issue here. What we do know is that as significant as this work is (US R&D expenditures were projected to top $580 billion across all sectors in 2018) and as large as the science/science-related workforce might be, the number of individuals actively engaged in such work makes up only a small fraction of the overall workforce in the United States, possibly as low as 3 percent of all workers (but certainly not more than 9 percent).[25] Furthermore, as we saw, the number of beginning high school students who are likely to make it through the science-training pipeline and end up in any of these various jobs is itself only around 7 percent. In any given science classroom of 25 first-year students, in other words, a teacher might count on one or maybe two students going on to get an associate's or bachelor's degree in a science-related field and then using that knowledge in their work.

Knowing this, it makes little sense to steer pre-college science education (or even introductory college science education for that matter) strongly in the direction of science-related workforce training. Such technical, content-centered teaching would benefit only a small number of students. And even then, the benefits appear to be limited to the individuals' career prospects; there is little or no evidence that increasing the science knowledge of high school students generally has any significant payoff in terms of the nation's economic growth or prosperity.

More important, though, and this is so much more important, a technical-training emphasis in high school science teaching would poorly serve the vast majority of students—the 93 percent or so who aren't going to graduate from high school or go on to a higher degree, or eventually take a job in a technical field. What about their needs and interests? This percentage alone easily tilts the arguments for science education away from the tier 1 technical-training goal and heavily toward the *science-for-general-education* goal, which we'll begin to explore in Chapter 4.

CHAPTER 4

THE FAILURE OF SCIENTIFIC LITERACY

Coming up with an effective approach to science education for the non-scientist has been a perennial challenge for educators and policymakers in the United States. Indeed, this is undoubtedly true for most advanced industrial countries across the globe. If technical training is set aside as the primary goal, as I argued it should be in Chapter 3, what should the focus of science teaching be for all those students who aren't bound for science-related higher education and work? From the arguments covered in this book so far, we have a variety of options to consider: science education for personal utility, democratic participation, better thinking, and cultural appreciation. It may be that all of these goals can be reasonably addressed in a well-designed science curriculum—or maybe not.

Complicating the picture of science education for the non-scientist is the notion of scientific literacy, an idea introduced in the United States after World War II as a catch-all for many of these *science-for-general-education* goals. Scientific literacy was, in fact, the second framing of an approach to science education for the lay public. The first came earlier in the twentieth century with the arrival of an entirely new school subject called "general science." Its designers built this course as something distinct from the traditional disciplinary subjects of biology, chemistry, and physics with the intent of helping students learn the general-thinking skill of problem solving that they could apply to situations in their daily lives. That problem-solving skill was later folded into the grab-bag of things that many counted as markers of being scientifically literate.

Since its introduction into the education landscape, scientific literacy has changed considerably in what it has stood for over the years, emphasizing goals related to culture, thinking, utility, and democracy in varying portions and combinations from one era to the next. On the one hand, the expansive nature of the construct has been effective at shining a spotlight on the general-education goals of science teaching. At the same time, though, in its amorphous, shape-shifting quality, the concept of scientific literacy has distracted us from a more careful consideration of the specific goals that science education might accomplish for the non-science-bound students, students who—as we've seen—make up over 90 percent of the enrollment in our nation's science classrooms. Once we recognize that the idea of scientific literacy serves no useful purpose, we can turn our attention to the underlying goals themselves.

* * *

The first effort to match science teaching to the needs of the general public was launched around 1910. Over the dozen years or so before then, educators (and some scientists) worried about the increasingly abstract knowledge that came with the professionalization of American science. One commentator noted that it was unfortunate that the formative years of science education

were "contemporaneous with the tendency of scientists generally to indulge in a spree of specialization."[1] The more scientists
prioritized advanced research, often in new state-of-the-art laboratories, the more science seemed to retreat from the ordinary
affairs of life. Average citizens found it difficult to grasp the complex theories and sophisticated mathematics they encountered,
however infrequently. Some felt this disconnect was responsible
for the declining enrollments in high school science courses at
the time, a situation that began to panic members of the scientific
community. One science educator complained that "from top to
bottom and from bottom to top, the science work in our educational institutions is chiefly shaped and planned to furnish a direct
path for the training of research workers." It was no wonder this
didn't fit "the great mass of humanity [that] have slight need of
such special training and technique."[2]

A small group of reformers took tentative steps toward a new
approach that would present science in a way that was more connected with the everyday interests of students. These reformers
piloted a smattering of survey courses that consisted of a year-long
patchwork of the established subjects of physics, biology, phys-
iography, and whatnot. By the middle of the decade, those survey courses had coalesced into the new school subject called "general science"—a course designed to meet the needs of students
where they lived rather than "to produce the scientist" as seemed
to be the goal of the more specialized courses.[3] What ultimately
emerged as the defining thread of the general-science movement
was an emphasis on problem solving drawn from Dewey's writing
on how people think—what became, for most science teachers,
the familiar steps of the scientific method.

The everyday issues students encountered rarely came packaged as "physics," "chemistry," or "biology" problems. Reformers deemed the subject-specific technical knowledge of the various disciplines mostly superfluous in addressing these issues. In the eyes of the general-science advocates, the most useful skill to be learned in a science class was an effective method for overcoming those everyday challenges—the scientific method. This powerful cognitive tool transcended disciplinary boundaries. It was something that the non-science-bound students (which was then most of the students of the time, as it is today) would surely find helpful in whatever endeavor they pursued, in work or play or in their homes or communities.[4]

The general-science course surged in popularity during the first half of the twentieth century. However, there was a sense among science educators—and increasingly among scientists as well—that the one-off course, popular as it was, didn't do enough to provide the public understanding that many felt was desperately needed. This was especially the case following the dramatic scientific accomplishments that emerged during World War II. Calls for a new "scientific literacy" began to surface in scientific journals, magazines, and newspapers around that time, far earlier than is generally recognized in science education circles. In 1945, for example, the Princeton physicist Gaylord Harnwell insisted that "the achievement of a broad scientific literacy is a long range undertaking of the greatest importance" in a "world in which science lies at the very roots of community, and a mastery of scientific thinking grows more and more indispensable."[5] During these years, the rising stature and importance of science prompted a rediscovery, or at least a renewed appreciation, of the science education needs of the average citizen. In the guise of scientific literacy, those perceived needs ebbed and flowed over time, mirroring the primary concerns about science and society right up to the present.

In the immediate postwar years, when it seemed that the success of the scientific enterprise might decide the fate of the nation, ideas about scientific literacy centered on what might be called the democratic-cultural argument. Scientists were in short supply, and their expertise was crucial to national security. If the public failed to recognize their unique societal role—and vote to support the research they did—dire consequences might very well result. "Developing scientific literacy among *all* the students" was essential, insisted the National Science Teachers Association executive director Robert Carleton. As he saw it in 1951, the primary question was "how can we help the young people of today, the voters of tomorrow, become informed so that they can make intelligent decisions?" Those voters, he explained, "will be the ones to determine in future years whether scientific endeavors are to flourish or wither."[6]

One thing Carleton deemed necessary was a 1950s style of cultural consciousness—the average person needed to learn, in his words, "what kind of breed of cat the scientist is." Knowing that (among other things) would help maintain the necessary public support. In the "manpower vs. manpower struggle with the forces of tyranny, the odds may be all against us." But for now, he claimed, our "scientific and technical 'know how' . . . gives us definite superiority." Our job is to "keep it that way." Promoting an appreciation of scientific culture—of who scientists were and what science was all about—among the lay public was the way to do that. This was the mid-century version of scientific literacy.[7]

By the early 1970s, moral uncertainty surrounding the activities of the military–scientific–industrial complex along with growing concerns about environmental pollution, the energy crisis, inequality, and other social ills prompted a revised conception of what it meant to be literate in science. No longer was the goal to have the public understand only the rarified culture of science, to appreciate an intellectual way of life that seemed so distant from the everyday world; efforts were now needed to temper rising public criticism of science and its social impact—what science seemed to be *doing* to the world.

In a piece he wrote for the *American Scientist* in 1971, NSF director William McElroy lamented that a growing segment of the public saw science "associated with terrible weapons of war, with pollution of air and water, with hazards to health and well-being." We need science education, he went on, to begin to "examine the relationships among science, technology, and society." The definition of scientific literacy now included this new element—a recognition of the harmful effects and limitations of the scientific enterprise. Science needed to be humanized, and the NSF launched a "science literacy" initiative to meet that need.[8]

It soon became apparent that the scientific literacy label could be stretched to cover a range of science-related learning outcomes. In 1966, science-education researchers at the University of Wisconsin combed through an assortment of science and science-education journals. They identified learning goals related to science and society, science and ethics, the nature of science, and science and technology as all falling under that heading. A decade later, University of Pennsylvania astrophysicist Benjamin Shen published an influential summary of the construct. He outlined what he saw as its three distinct forms: practical science literacy (using science to improve living conditions), civic science literacy (understanding enough science to participate in democratic decision-making), and cultural science literacy (appreciating science as a human achievement). And in 1983, the journal *Daedalus*, the founding editor of which was the Harvard physicist Gerald Holton, devoted its entire spring issue to the topic, with articles exploring the connections between science and democratic theory, economic productivity, and education reform, among others.[9]

Through the 1980s, scientific literacy meant nearly anything and everything. Science advocates, education reformers, and policymakers voiced concerns about science, technology, and society (now with genetic engineering, toxic-waste sites, and the hole in the ozone layer thrown into the mix). They worried that the public lacked the basic levels of scientific understanding necessary (though rarely specified) for making policy decisions, and expressed anxieties about the average person's knowledge of basic science content, seemingly just because. Calls for more and better science education to improve scientific literacy were made in the same breath with statements about preparing "highly trained specialists, such as engineers, electronics experts, and energy scientists" to meet the nation's expanding technical workforce needs. Scientific literacy seemed in these times to extend even beyond the non-science-bound average citizen, especially when the country needed to face the growing economic threat posed by automobile and consumer-electronic imports from Japan and South Korea.[10]

Amid the public angst over the country's desperate need for scientific literacy, researchers perhaps not surprisingly began to try to measure it. The effort to devise a test or scale of everyday science knowledge wasn't completely new. One of the first attempts occurred as far back as 1919 when a University of Chicago researcher, believing that some minimum level of science knowledge was necessary for essential life functions, developed what he called a "range of information test" in science. It wasn't until the 1970s, though, that the idea of systematic, standardized assessments of science knowledge gained significant traction. The first of these to make a splash was the National Assessment of Educational Progress (NAEP), commonly referred to as the "nation's report card." Results publicized in 1975 highlighted a decline in science scores among all age levels (from 9 to 17 year olds) between 1969 and 1973. Although the science portion of the NAEP test purported to measure four main areas, including science process skills and understanding of the nature of science, most of the test items focused on knowledge of facts and principles. The results were less than encouraging.[11]

In the late 1970s, public-opinion expert Jon Miller and his colleagues began surveying a representative sample of American adults every two years to gauge their general level of scientific literacy. Developed with funding from the National Science Foundation, the survey measured understanding of the scientific method, knowledge of basic facts, and appreciation of science's social impact. By the 1980s, the survey had evolved to consist of, in part, a series of true–false or simple selection questions. Subjects were asked, for example, whether "the oxygen we breathe comes from plants," if "the center of the earth is very hot," whether "electrons are smaller than atoms," and if light travels faster than sound. The key operational definition of scientific literacy here was the ability of an individual to understand simple science facts. As Miller explained, "the scientifically literate should understand the scientific method and vocabulary well enough to follow public debates about issues involving science and technology." The survey results didn't paint a rosy picture; reported levels of adult scientific literacy hovered around the 5–7 percent range, and the press was quick to spotlight the dismal numbers.[12]

The US National Science Board (NSB) featured Miller's scientific-literacy work in the 1989 edition of its *Science and Engineering Indicators*, the biennial report launched in 1972 during the height of the anti-science years in America, and has included it in every issue since. Over the years, the NSB version of scientific literacy has remained more or less constant. It meant "knowing basic facts and concepts about science and having an understanding of how science works" (this latter point being measured by only a few questions about experimental design and probability)— an awfully thin view of what it might mean to be literate in science.

Thin as it might be, the NSB's focus on scientific literacy as essentially a vocabulary test was well aligned with the cultural-literacy-inspired version popularized by the physicist James Trefil and his colleague, geologist Robert Hazen, in the early 1990s. For them, scientific literacy was just "a mix of facts, vocabulary, concepts, history and philosophy."[13] If you could understand the science stories in the news, you were scientifically literate according to them. Both Hazen and Trefil and the NSB were—and are—operating within the version of the democratic argument for science education that sees concept familiarity as the minimal threshold for meaningful participation in civic affairs.

THE FAILURE OF SCIENTIFIC LITERACY

So, where does this leave scientific literacy as a goal of science education? Nowhere helpful, I'm afraid. As we have seen, advocates have used the idea of scientific literacy as a vague placeholder for a variety of science-education learning outcomes for the lay public since the 1940s. Starting out as a way to describe how an informed citizen might come to see and appreciate the key role of science and scientists in the new postwar scientific age, it quickly expanded to include the societal implications of science and technology during a period of declining status. It was even stretched to subsume technical-workforce-training goals in the 1980s during the height of the first wave of global economic competition from Japan.

At the other end of the spectrum, the emergence of scientific-literacy measures by Miller and his colleagues and, more recently, the international assessments of science achievement from the likes of TIMSS and PISA have effectively hijacked the concept of scientific literacy with something that has reduced it to "that which can be tested," which typically ends up assessing the recall of basic facts (despite efforts to get at more complex understandings). As we've seen, though, some believe that the facts are all you need.

To argue then that the goal of science education should be scientific literacy for American youth, given this history, is to argue for nothing specific at all. This appears to be the conclusion of the most recent assessment of the concept made by a committee of the National Academies of Science, Engineering, and Medicine.[14] Is the goal mastery of content knowledge for students to participate in the global economy? Is it an awareness of the complex interrelationships between science and society? Or is it some appreciation of the culture of science and how humans come to know the natural world? To say, "yes, all those things are what it means to be scientifically literate!" simply avoids the more important question about what science education can and should *actually* accomplish. It would be far better to just get rid of the concept of scientific literacy altogether and instead ask the underlying questions about what the real goals of science education should be—specifically.

CHAPTER 5

HOW WELL DOES "THE SCIENCE EDUCATION WE HAVE" ACTUALLY WORK?

Up to this point, we have established two things pretty clearly. The first is that, although technical training is a legitimate goal of science education (this being essentially the utilitarian argument at the national level), it doesn't seem to be the best fit for the majority of students in our schools. Think back to our ninth graders, only 7 percent of whom ended up making it through the pipeline, earning a degree, and working in a science-related field. The second is that the way we normally talk about the non-technical-training goals of science education isn't very useful. All of these general-education-in-science goals have been lumped into the catch-all concept "scientific literacy." And, given that it has been used to refer to nearly every possible goal of science education, it offers no meaningful way to make sense of why *specifically* we might want to teach science to the general public.

The next step in our analysis is to examine those general-education goals and see how they stack up in terms of meeting the needs of the majority of our ninth graders. That's what the bulk of this chapter will be about—taking a hard look at what we actually know about how the person on the street draws upon, thinks about, or uses science in their everyday affairs. We'll approach this both from an individual and a societal perspective. Looking carefully at the empirical evidence we have on this question is the heart of this chapter. Indeed, it is a central theme of the book as a whole. What we find is that many of the foundational assumptions that scientists, science educators, policymakers, and local community leaders make about how science-content and science-process knowledge function in our everyday decision-making are just plain wrong. We need to acknowledge this clearly and unequivocally if we hope to make science education something truly worth pursuing in our public schools.

We should begin our analysis by looking at the science education we have. In other words, let's accept the fact that policymakers, parents, and local school leaders—despite their hand waving at democratic participation, better-thinking skills, or what have you—have defaulted to the technical-training goal of science education or, if not that, simply assume that mastering scientific facts, principles, textbook problem solutions, and assorted laboratory techniques are the basis for all the science-for-general-education goals that so many have gathered under the broader concept of scientific literacy. After all, this is what high school students seem to be spending most of their time learning—the internal, traditional content of the various science disciplines.[1] The question that we need to ask then is "Does this kind of learning help students realize the science-for-general-education goals that everyone says we typically get from high-quality science instruction?"

Science Education for Everyday Problems

Let's begin with the *personal utility* goal—the idea that scientific facts can be useful in helping individuals navigate everyday challenges. The belief that knowing how the world works might come in handy in various personal situations is intuitively appealing, to be sure. This is what Stephen Forbes referred to back in the nineteenth century when he wrote that "the lot of the countryman and of the workmen in towns would be ameliorated if they knew more of the facts and laws of matter and of life."[2]

Many science teachers I know have spun all sorts of hypothetical examples in response to the perennial student question— "How is this useful?" Being science teachers, they naturally see science everywhere and so might connect concepts such as pressure, friction, translational and rotational velocity, and Bernoulli's principle to the physics of throwing a curveball in baseball, for example. The problem is that, while it's true that most everything around us can be explained or analyzed through some scientific lens, the decisions we make and actions we take in the situations we regularly find ourselves in are rarely informed by scientific content knowledge. Although the physics of pitching can be fascinating, a pitcher doesn't draw on any understanding of physics to strike out opposing players. This is the argument against science for personal utility in a nutshell—we rarely use scientific knowledge to guide our in-the-moment actions.

Most people live their lives, in fact, largely oblivious to the concepts and principles of science. The average person may have learned quite a bit of science in school or even college, but they often forget what they've learned once they close the textbook and take that last exam. Researchers have shown that students routinely forget significant amounts of the content knowledge covered in any given class. In one study, for example, researchers saw that senior physics majors scored 60 percent lower on a written assessment of material they learned four years earlier during their freshman year. The fall-off was similar among second-year medical students in another study that found that after five to eleven months, the students retained only about 60 percent of the basic science content they learned during their first year of school.[3] Surely the passage of even greater lengths of time than what elapsed in these studies (and the fact that most of us aren't science majors) makes it even less likely that such knowledge stays with us. How much do any of us as adults remember the details of what we learned in our high school science classes?

Perhaps the most damning evidence that the science we learn in school fails to stick, though, is found in the biennial test of scientific literacy tracked in the National Science Board's *Science and Engineering Indicators*. In the most recent assessment of public understanding of basic scientific facts, researchers found that only 72 percent of individuals knew that the Earth goes around the Sun (and not the Sun around the Earth), just 46 percent knew that electrons are smaller than atoms, and only half knew that antibiotics work only on bacteria and not viruses. After decades of efforts and hundreds of millions of dollars earmarked to improve science education in the United States, people don't appear to recall even the most basic science facts after leaving school, results that must be frustrating indeed.[4]

One reason for this lack of retention is that science content is largely taught in isolation from everyday problems and experiences. It simply doesn't meaningfully intersect with how people live their lives—the days go by just the same, whether it's the Sun orbiting the Earth or the Earth orbiting the Sun. But even if we did retain all the content we learned in school, it still wouldn't help us all that much. That is because either we've already learned from experience how to navigate those situations in which science knowledge might be useful or the situations are so complicated it's not obvious how what we might have learned in school would apply.

Consider all that we know from our direct interactions with the world. These everyday experiences give us immediate feedback that quickly teaches us what we need to know. A pitcher masters the curveball by repeatedly throwing—or trying to throw—one. The resulting strikeout is the measure of whether the pitch was a success. From a young age, we know not to put our hands in a flame because of the pain that comes from the burn. These various experiences not only provide an immediate stimulus–response form of learning but also contribute to the natural development of what psychologists call *intuitive theories,* which are informal, self-generated ways that we make sense of and navigate various aspects of the natural world.[5]

In the recent book *Scienceblind,* the cognitive psychologist Andrew Shtulman describes the pervasive and enduring gap that exists between our intuitive theories and the corresponding accepted scientific understandings of the world. In our everyday experience with moving objects, for example, most people operate with what's called an impetus theory of motion—the idea that when someone throws a ball, they impart the force of the throw (the impetus) into the ball, and that force carries the ball along until it "wears out," at which point the ball falls to the ground. From a Newtonian perspective, one would say the ball accelerates with the force of the thrower's arm and, after its release, continues in motion, with its initial velocity slowly decreasing due to the friction from the air, tracing a parabolic path as the force of gravity draws the ball toward the ground.

Shtulman details many of the intuitive theories psychologists have identified—the idea that heat acts like a fluid (caloric theory), that air has no mass, that a biological species is defined by an ideal type rather than by a population of individuals, and so many more—and shows how resistant these are to formal instruction. One study Shtulman describes looked at a group of students who had successfully solved thousands of textbook physics problems over the course of two years and yet still retained their intuitive theories of motion. The only effect solving all those physics problems in class had on those students was to improve their ability to solve more physics problems; it did little to move them toward a conceptual understanding of motion as viewed through the eyes of a physicist.[6]

The takeaway from this is that humans are pretty darn good at getting along in their day-to-day practical affairs without science. Not knowing the accepted scientific concepts and theories of heat, motion, mass, gravity, and so on doesn't seem to matter all that much. As the authors of one article on intuitive theories remark, our amazing *lack* of knowledge "stands in stark contrast to the proficiency and ease with which we navigate our everyday lives."[7] We learn to be careful on icy sidewalks, learn not to burn ourselves taking brownies out of the oven, and can even learn to throw a curveball (with practice) without formal knowledge of friction, kinetic theories of heat, and aerodynamics. It's not that our intuitive theories of the world are "right." But they do seem to be good enough to help us get by in the world safely and successfully.

The fact that whole civilizations flourished for centuries before current scientific understandings were even developed says something about how necessary formal scientific knowledge really is for daily life.

So, if we rely on experience to manage the mundane things in our lives, how do we handle the more complex situations we encounter? Let's say you are trying to remove a parking sticker from the inside of your car's windshield. You've peeled away the sticker itself, but you're left with the sticky gunk on the glass that won't easily come off. A high school chemistry teacher might excitedly jump up to explain how the material they covered in that unit on organic solvents would give you everything you need to know to clean the window properly. But, given the data on student retention, would you even remember the details of what was covered back then? And even if you did remember, would that knowledge *obviously* help you with the problem at hand? What exactly is the chemical composition of that gunk? What solvent would be the best to use? Do you have to worry about the solvent damaging the dashboard if some of it drips on it as you try to clean the window? What is a typical dashboard even made out of? There are so many unknowns here with what seems to be a simple problem.

What about a situation that's more complex and has greater potential consequence for your personal safety? Suppose you've become eligible for a new vaccine against some more lethal variant of COVID-19 and are unsure whether you should get it. Little of the content you learned in your high school biology class is likely to be of much help. Maybe you remember something about viruses—they inject DNA into your cells and take them over (or something like that). And you covered the immune system.

But that was a long time ago—things about T-cells, antibodies, antigens, and an immune response. The decision in front of you is whether to get vaccinated. And then, what if the only choice is something like the Johnson & Johnson vaccine. Is it possible that you'll get those blood clots you've read about? Is one shot better than two, or worse?

The way people typically make decisions in situations like these isn't to rely on what they learned in their high school science classes. Indeed, researchers generally agree that the public understanding of science is severely limited in both depth and breadth. A necessary consequence of this is that individuals seek out information from trusted sources as needed—from friends, family members, teachers, medical professionals, online information outlets, the public library. Finding out the easiest way to clean the sticker gunk off the windshield turns out to be as simple as watching a YouTube video or posting a question to an online automobile discussion forum. The decision about the vaccine is perhaps less straightforward. How it gets made will have more to do with the particular social network one belongs to. What people decide to do, particularly about issues that are socially, politically, and intellectually complex, is heavily influenced by what they read and who they regularly interact with. Are your friends and family members getting vaccinated? If they are, you likely will too.[8]

Some might argue that understanding the basic science concepts from school is a necessary baseline to begin to have those conversations with the people in your network or to process what we read in the news or encounter in social media. This is true. However, the level of understanding required is truly minimal, nothing more really than a familiarity with a small list of vocabulary words like atom, radiation, DNA, chromosome, heat, temperature, and so on. This is what Trefil means when he says that the public needs to know enough science to "enter the debate" when science-related social issues come to the fore. Much of this vocabulary we pick up in the course of our natural language development and everyday social interactions. We learn it in school as well. But we don't rely on any deep understanding of these terms and concepts to make important decisions in our lives. It remains the case that most members of the general public, as we saw, walk around with very little understanding of the science taught in school. What we do know is that the decisions individuals make— whatever their level of science understanding—are more likely to be influenced by their social networks and trusted sources than by the science content they may or may not remember from high school.[9]

Science Education for Democratic Decision-Making

Given what we've found with respect to the *personal utility* goal, we shouldn't be too optimistic about how a content-focused/technical -training approach to science education would prepare students to deal with issues in the democratic-participation domain. After all, the situations are just as, if not more, complex. Here we have challenges like human-induced climate change, global pandemics, autonomous driving technologies, human gene editing, science research funding, local land-use decisions, and on and on. Such science-related civic issues go well beyond the impacts they might have on any particular individual. By definition, civic issues have some bearing on *all* of our lives or those of some smaller group of individuals. Given their comparatively broad impact, they require a collective response or decision—the development of policy, the passage and enactment of legislation, or a decision by a town council, school board, or some other representative body. These are, in other words, science-related problems in which the public has a *shared* interest that requires resolution through democratic deliberation.[10]

Take the issue of vaccination. Considering whether you or your child should be vaccinated falls under the personal utility argument. Whatever you decide about that, your decision impacts only you or your family member (leaving aside questions of what the aggregation of many individual decisions like this might mean for the community). A democratic-participation version of the issue would be whether a school district should require *all* children to be vaccinated in order to attend school or whether the federal government should mandate vaccinations for all federal workers and contractors. The issue at one level seems to be the same (the vaccine's safety and its efficacy in preventing disease). However, there's more to consider in setting public policy. For one, knowledge beyond a vaccine's effect on individual health is needed. Officials would want to know about the community transmission of the disease in question, the capacity of healthcare facilities to manage the sick, and which mitigation strategies are likely to be most effective in a given population. The possibility of enforcing a blanket requirement that affects all children or workers in a community goes well beyond an individual's immediate personal concerns.

Another example might involve the consideration of a federal carbon tax to address the threat of global climate change. Members of Congress need to know the science before making any such policy decision. Would reducing carbon emissions from factories and automobiles via a legislative approach of this kind significantly lower atmospheric carbon-dioxide levels? How certain are we about current trends in CO_2 emissions? What do we know about the projected effects on climate and the frequency of severe local weather events? Do we know enough collectively to pass legislation that would significantly alter how we all live and how our economy functions? What falls within the range of possible outcomes if the government fails to act?

There are hundreds of science-related social issues like this that require some form of democratic deliberation for their resolution, everything from federal regulation of stem-cell research to local decisions about the designation of wetlands. All are just as complex as the complex problems described in the personal-utility examples. What was true about the usefulness of science-content knowledge for those is equally true for all of these. Whether someone is a U.S. senator, representative, city alderperson, or school board member, decisions about science-related issues in democratic bodies are unlikely to be informed only by the facts and concepts learned in school science classes, at least not how they have long been and are currently being taught. Deliberative bodies, instead, draw on an assortment of social networks and information sources. This includes hearing expert testimony, carefully reading policy briefs, and considering input from constituents and lobbyists. Voters do the same on matters of significance to them, tapping their trusted networks and doing their own due diligence in gathering the information they need to make various decisions about science-related matters.

Where does school content knowledge fit in all this? It doesn't really. Over the past twenty years or so, studies have shown that when people are asked to deliberate over what researchers in science education call "socioscientific issues"—such as climate change, genetic engineering, nanotechnology, and so on—they rely primarily on social, moral, ideological, or ethical factors in coming to a decision. Although individuals may draw upon science-content knowledge in certain circumstances (if explicitly prompted to or if learned just prior to consideration of a particular issue), more typically they don't have the science-content knowledge ready at hand to apply (the problem with retention), find the relevant science content difficult to make sense of, or don't see its relevance. Rather they proceed intuitively, without deliberate, rational analysis, invoking personal, affective criteria in arriving at what they believe to be the appropriate resolution. Research in the field of science communication has arrived at a similar conclusion, finding that science literacy (defined as knowledge of science content) "has only a limited role in shaping public perceptions and decisions."[11]

Some have argued that more and better science learning is the way to address these seeming deficiencies among the public. However, improving science-content knowledge would hardly ensure more objective and thoughtful deliberation about science-related issues. In fact, studies have found that individuals with relatively high levels of science-content knowledge routinely ignore scientific evidence that contradicts their pre-established beliefs or selectively draw on that content to support their biases and preconceived arguments.[12] In one particularly compelling study, Yale researcher Dan Kahan and his colleagues found that increased levels of scientific literacy among individuals (as measured by the National Science Foundation *Science and Engineering Indicators* assessments developed by Jon Miller) were correlated with higher levels of political and cultural polarization. Group identity has far more influence on how one decides controversial science-related issues than content-based scientific literacy does. "For ordinary citizens," Kahan and his colleagues conclude, "the reward for acquiring greater scientific knowledge and more reliable technical-reasoning capacities is a greater facility to discover and use—or explain away—evidence relating to their groups' positions."[13]

Science Education for Culture

Of all the science-for-general-education goals, the aim of teaching science to promote cultural awareness and appreciation is perhaps the easiest to assess. The reason for this is simple. It's not a goal anyone is trying to reach right now. Few efforts can be found in mainstream science classrooms to promote any understanding of the interconnections and reciprocal influences between science and the broader culture among middle and high school students.

In the AP courses increasingly being adopted in the country's high school science programs, for example, little if any attention is given to topics that might help students see the deep interconnections among the various disciplinary fields in the sciences or how science has influenced (and has been influenced) by the culture in which we all live. None of the instructional units described in the guides put out by the College Board (the company that runs the AP program) for any of their courses in biology, physics, chemistry, and environmental science make any meaningful references to material related to the history of science, the intersections between science and society, or how our understandings of the natural world have influenced humanity. All the

AP courses appear to begin and end with the technical content of the disciplines, which in itself might not be a problem if not for the fact that these courses are taking over more and more of the high school science curriculum.

While discussions of cultural connections are far more likely to show up in textbooks written for standard, non-AP high school science courses, they are typically included as a sidebar or treated only briefly in a chapter's introduction to add a bit of humanistic flavor. Rarely are explorations of, say, the impact of Darwin's theory of evolution on our understanding of the place of humans in the natural world or how Newton's universal theory of gravitation joined the physics of the heavens and Earth in a new worldview made the focus of instruction in these books. The textbooks of today—and the teaching that inevitably flows from them—offer the usual rundown of the common facts, concepts, and theories of the traditional school science subjects. A book like Holton and Rutherford's *Project Physics* from the 1970s, which walked students through the historical development of some of the most profound ideas in science (how Galileo's work on falling bodies, for example, challenged the widely held Aristotelean cosmology of the time) or examined the societal impact of technologies of electrification in the 1930s, would be a clear outlier in the school science curriculum landscape of our current era.[14]

The science education standards provide more of the same. While the first stab at a nationwide set of goals for student learning—launched with the American Association for the Advancement of Science's Project 2061 in 1989—included explorations of history and philosophy, intersections of science with political and economic systems, and discussions of the cultural effects on human behavior alongside the standard disciplinary science-content knowledge, the most recent version of science standards (the Next Generation Science Standards) that guide most school programs these days contains almost none of these things. In the 102-page NGSS topic list, there are no mentions of culture or history (other than the geologic history of the Earth). There are zero mentions of Darwin, Galileo, Dalton, Einstein, Curie, Watson, Crick, or Rosalind Franklin. Newton comes up only in connection with the various laws of motion associated with his name, and connections between science and society are described predominantly within the cross-cutting concept of the "Influence of Engineering, Technology, and Science on Society and the Natural World." There one finds topics such as risk mitigation, cost-benefit analysis, and use of technology to meet human needs—topics that encompass a limited and rather managerial/economic view of the science–society interface.[15] The verdict on this particular argument for science education is unambiguous—the science education we have right now simply ignores the goal of cultural understanding.

Science Education for Future Scientists and Engineers (An Aside on Technical Training)

Although this chapter is about how well the content-focused science education we have matches up with the science-for-general education goals described in Chapter 1, I would like to circle back for a moment to the technical-training argument. After getting to the end of this chapter, some of you might be thinking that, despite me showing that the science education we have doesn't do much to meet any of these general-education goals, perhaps it's still pretty good for the 7 percent heading off to science-related degrees and jobs, right? Maybe you're still not convinced that the number is only 7 percent, or maybe you think that that 7 percent is the key to the country's economic future, and so we would be right to place our emphasis there for the good of everyone. Even if this were the case, would the default approach to science education actually prepare our students for these types of careers?

The answer to this question is—we don't really know. There's plenty of evidence, in fact, to suggest that this may very well not be the best way to train individuals to enter the technical workforce. Recall that most students forget a good deal of what they are taught in traditional content-focused science classes once those final exams are wrapped up. The physics and medical students described earlier retained only about half of what they learned in their science courses. And such students, even if they do remember what they've learned, often will revert to intuitive explanations of natural phenomena in non-school settings.

In one famous study (famous at least in science education circles), graduates of Harvard University (some of whom were physics majors), when asked what causes the change of the seasons, offered explanations completely at odds with accepted scientific understandings. They insisted that the seasons cycled with the changing distance between the Earth and Sun. That is, we get summer when the Earth is warmed by the Sun as it draws near, and winter when the Sun is furthest away—which is incorrect (it's the tilt of the Earth toward the Sun that matters). The result was similar when they were asked about the phases of the Moon, which they claimed were caused by clouds blocking portions of what we can see, leaving only a portion of the Moon visible, resulting in the various phases (half, crescent, or new moon). In each instance, these students relied more on their intuitions than on the high school and college-level science coursework they had taken.[16]

The value of science-content mastery for future scientists has also been thrown into doubt by no less an authority than the Nobel Prize-winning physicist Carl Wieman. Wieman has made a second career out of studying how college students best learn science. He has frequently expressed his frustration with graduate students who possess top grades and test scores but, nonetheless, struggle to be productive in the laboratory. Many of them know the content, he admitted, but are "not able to identify and solve actual scientific problems."[17] All this is to say that the traditional approach to science teaching may very well not be the best route to scientific and technical innovation.

* * *

So, where do things stand at this point? We know that the default approach to science education both historically and currently is to focus on teaching the facts and principles of science, that is, *science-content knowledge*. It's been this way because such an approach is easiest for teachers to teach and because society has moved toward the technical-training goal in response to both the greater emphasis on science as an engine of economic growth and accountability systems based on standards and standardized assessment, which are inherently geared toward content mastery. With respect to the science-for-general-education goals outlined in earlier chapters, this approach almost completely fails. Whether it would be used for personal utility or democratic decision-making, science-content knowledge—even if it were retained for any appreciable length of time—simply does not map onto the way people make sense of and interact with the world in their daily lives.

CHAPTER 6

SCIENCE FOR BETTER THINKING AND THE LIMITS OF "DOING" SCIENCE

If the default, content-focused approach to science education offers little to help us manage everyday personal challenges and guide our democratic decision-making and nothing at all to foster the cultural appreciation of science, we'd be hard-pressed to see any positive contribution to better general-thinking skills. Yet, oddly enough, scientists and science educators regularly appeal to this learning goal when they talk about what they hope their students will gain from their teaching. As we've seen, the goal of science education for better thinking has a long and storied career in the history of science education. This was one of the central aims articulated by Project 2061 back in the 1980s as project members shared their worries about the persistence of "the irrational in American life."[1] The scientific mindset was and often is viewed as the epitome of enlightenment rationality. Looking at where science education is today, however, such talk appears to be nothing more than wishful thinking, the most obvious reason being that the process of science (like science for cultural appreciation) is rarely taught in our default technical-training approach to science education, and when it is, it isn't taught very well.

Of all the efforts to engage students in the process of science over the years, the most intensive effort came during the national-security crisis of the 1950s and 1960s. Spurred by the hysteria over Sputnik, the National Science Foundation enlisted top scientists in physics, chemistry, biology, and other disciplines to develop up-to-date textbooks and curriculum materials that would provide students opportunities to engage in the process of science or, as they called it, scientific inquiry. With these new curriculum materials—developed by groups such as the Physical Science Study Committee and the Biological Sciences Curriculum Study—and an influx of federal funds aimed at improving school science laboratory facilities and equipment, these reformers believed they might realize the promise of students deeply learning science through the experience of doing science.

Even with the massive investment of time, expertise, and tax dollars, the initiative largely failed. Follow-up studies conducted by NSF to gauge the long-range impact of this work found that teachers had reverted to (or never abandoned) traditional methods of instruction focused on textbook reading, lectures, and problem sets. Scientific inquiry was nowhere to be found.[2]

Despite the evident failures of the Sputnik-era reforms, a new wave of science educators pushed for the resurrection of inquiry-based instruction in the 1990s during the dawn of the standards era. Such is the power of this belief in doing science to learn science. Concerns over America's economic security seemed to call for a renewed commitment to having students engage in "authentic" scientific activities. The National Science Education Standards, published in 1996, made inquiry the centerpiece of its standards-based pedagogy, featuring it as the preferred instructional method and as one of the key learning goals. In other words, the authors hoped that students would both do science and, as a result, under-stand science primarily as a process of exploration rather than as an assemblage of content knowledge.

Not surprisingly, teaching science this way never really got off the ground. Studies on the impact of the science standards found that the push to hold students accountable to more and more science facts forced teachers to abandon time-intensive inquiry methods (if they ever took them up in the first place).

Things haven't improved over time. A 2013 study examining the presence of inquiry teaching among a group of highly motivated, well-qualified science teachers found few of them engaging their students in this sort of work. Given that the teachers in this study were those most likely to successfully implement inquiry-based teaching, the general state of affairs, the researchers noted, "may be even more dismal that it appears." This is a familiar story, one reaffirmed in the National Research Council's 2006 study of lab-oratory teaching, *America's Lab Report*, and again by Mehta and Fine's vain search for "deeper learning" most recently. School sci-ence instruction has failed time and again to meaningfully engage students in the process of science. Teachers, it seems, almost always fall back on content mastery as the primary learning objective.[3]

Much of the reason for this centers on the continuing chal-lenge of getting teachers to convey the essential nature of scien-tific inquiry to their students in some reasonably authentic way. It's something teachers are just not comfortable doing, mainly because few of them have had any direct experience with scien-tific research or reasoning themselves. As a result, many struggle to recognize what actual scientific inquiry even looks like, in or out of the classroom. Moreover, when science education faculty in teacher-education programs try to help teachers develop a deeper understanding of what scientific work genuinely entails, whether through carefully organized instruction or immersion in summer research experiences, the results are inevitably disappointing. Despite the targeted instruction and hands-on experience, teachers routinely revert to inaccurate "folk theories" of how science is done (invoking the five-step "scientific method" of bygone times) or return to traditional instructional approaches out of convenience.[4]

It might help if teachers had thoughtfully designed textbooks or other curriculum materials that they could rely on to help their students experience scientific inquiry in some authentic way, but efforts to develop such materials—despite the best intentions of curriculum developers—have failed to capture anything close to what scientists actually do in the process of their work. In one landmark study, researchers Clark Chinn and Betina Malhotra analyzed a wide range of student inquiry tasks found in school textbooks, trade books, educational software, and websites of science activities. They found that none of them came close to capturing the complex reasoning processes scientists engage in during research. Their conclusion was unequivocal. "Many scientific inquiry tasks given to students in schools," they wrote, "do not reflect the core attributes of authentic scientific reasoning." The school tasks were frequently oversimplified activities that had students conduct a predetermined experiment, observe and make a record of some natural phenomenon, or follow a set procedure that merely illustrated some scientific principle. There were few opportunities for students to pose their own questions, select variables to test and control, invent procedures to test their hypotheses, or deliberate with their peers on the outcome of experimental results. Not only were the school inquiry tasks far removed from actual scientific work, but the authors also concluded that, in fact, "the epistemology of many school inquiry tasks is *antithetical* to the epistemology of authentic science." In other words, it seems that doing "school science" in this way led to greater *mis*understandings of what science is and how it works than greater understanding.[5]

In the face of the difficulties classroom teachers and curriculum developers have had implementing meaningful inquiry teaching, the appeal of doing science to learn science persists among scientists, science education researchers, and policymakers. All appear to cling to the belief that somehow engaging in the process of science possesses some extraordinary pedagogical power. The committed believe that the natural result will be better, more rational thinking skills. Many have also signed on to the idea that doing science will result in rich understandings of the nature of science and will help students better learn disciplinary content as well (even if, as we've seen, the value of such learning is questionable).[6]

Of course, these assumed learning outcomes can't be tested in classrooms where inquiry isn't done or is done in some poor imitation of real science. There are, however, programs that operate outside of classrooms in genuine research settings that offer a way to see what individuals who participate in research actually learn working alongside professional scientists. The most common programs are summer research apprenticeships for teachers, undergraduate research experiences for college students, and "citizen-science" opportunities for people of all ages and backgrounds. All of these have risen in popularity over the past few decades based on the magical thinking that simply doing science in some form will redound to the educational benefit of the participants. But what have the studies of such programs found?

Let's do a quick rundown. Across studies conducted over the past twenty years, researchers report that evidence for the benefits of science research experiences is quite limited. Participants mostly learn things such as lab safety along with skills and technical procedures like culturing bacteria, collecting specimens, micro pipetting, and running data-analysis software—things specific to the research project on which they're working. All this makes perfect sense. Individuals joining a team for a brief period of time are often given well-defined tasks to perform. They are less likely to be invited to see the "big-picture" aspects of the project, such as what the guiding research questions are and how answers to those might fit into the ongoing stream of scientific work in that particular field. As a result, participants instead learn how long it takes to collect high-quality data, how tedious such work is, and the overall messiness of day-to-day life in the laboratory. As for whether these experiences impact understanding of science more broadly, the consensus is that they don't. As one researcher put it, understandings of the nature of science "do not seem to be significantly affected by apprenticeship experiences."[7]

A 2017 report drafted by a National Academy of Sciences committee provides perhaps the most accurate assessment of what can reasonably be expected from these kinds of participatory programs. After surveying the literature on this topic, it concluded that the primary goals of undergraduate research experiences are increasing participation and retention of STEM students, promoting disciplinary knowledge and practices, and integrating students into STEM culture. In other words, these student experiences appear to work primarily and most effectively as a form

of professional training. Although the committee made passing reference to preparing informed citizens who might become
"savvy consumer[s] of STEM information" or who "know how
to make informed decisions based on the strength of evidence,"
the focus throughout the report is squarely on the STEM career
pipeline. Comments about helping students develop skill in general, evidence-based reasoning strategies are just more of the
same aspirational goals touted by all science education advocates
over the years—always hoped for but rarely achieved. Indeed, the
report makes no reference to any empirical studies that deal with
student outcomes that fall outside the science-career-preparation
orbit.[8]

So, teachers don't typically teach the process of science in
schools; textbooks and curriculum materials misrepresent what
that process is; and working alongside scientists in a lab as part
of an immersive research experience offers little insight into the
big-picture of how science works, providing nothing more than
a kind of job shadowing or narrow technical training. Given all
this, it's fair to ask: What are the prospects that most students will
learn to think like scientists in a typical science classroom? The
short answer is—not good.

Research has shown that under ideal conditions, elementary-
level students do show proficiency in some aspects of scientific
reasoning. They can distinguish hypothetical beliefs from evidence. They can pick out controlled experiments from those that
have no apparent control. And they can engage in basic evaluation of data. One of the surprising findings from studies on
the development of scientific thinking among younger children
over the past few decades has been that children are far more

competent in these sorts of tasks than previously thought.[9] That said, they still struggle to create controlled experiments on their own, typically manipulate too many variables at once in a given experimental setup, cannot effectively evaluate arguments, and cling to prior beliefs in the face of conflicting evidence. Many of these same difficulties are found in adolescents and adults as well. There doesn't appear to be a natural developmental path toward higher levels of scientific reasoning, nor does there seem to be any obvious instructional strategies to help students easily learn the skills involved.[10]

The challenge is fairly obvious. Developing scientific reasoning in students is difficult because scientific reasoning itself is difficult. The eminent British developmental biologist Lewis Wolpert famously made this point in his 1993 book, *The Unnatural Nature of Science*. He explained that the towering achievements of science are so remarkable just *because* the thinking that led to them goes against the grain of common sense. Science "involves a special mode of thought." The "natural thinking" we typically engage in, he insisted, "will never give an understanding of the nature of science," because "scientific ideas are, with rare exceptions, counterintuitive." To arrive at such ideas requires a precise, deliberate, oftentimes quantitative way of thinking—a way of thinking so contrary to everyday cognition that it took thousands of years to emerge in the human species and requires years of intense training to develop even in scientists. As the authors of an assessment of the psychological underpinnings of scientific reasoning conclude, this kind of reasoning is simply not part of our equipment for everyday causal reasoning. No wonder it's so hard to teach.[11]

But, even if we could get students to master the processes of scientific reasoning through intensive, carefully structured learning experiences, would that ensure that the equation would come out as is so often assumed, that scientific reasoning leads to better everyday thinking? Might it be possible to realize the goal of the Project 2061 reformers to educate away the "irrational in American life"? Unfortunately, it's not likely. The problem of transfer—learning a skill in one domain with the expectation that one can easily apply it in another, unfamiliar domain—was recognized as far back as the early 1900s, and it's no less a problem today. Researchers have shown that even students who have successfully mastered the ability to control variables in an experiment (after sustained instruction) struggle to transfer that ability to novel problems—and that's with problems that, although new, are still essentially "science" problems.[12] When it comes to solving problems out in the real world, all bets are off.

The reason for this is that the "natural thinking" that people engage in on a daily basis that Wolpert talked about operates with a completely different set of cognitive skills and dispositions. Individuals approach everyday problems using intuitive shortcuts, heuristics, and emotions that are largely tacit and invoked unconsciously. We make gut-level decisions often without stopping to engage in careful, rational analysis. If we do stop and deliberate, such efforts are easily overwhelmed by emotion and personal bias. This kind of natural thinking—the product of thousands of years of evolution—is ingrained in how we engage with the world, and as a result, it's incredibly tough to overcome. Moreover, just like our intuitive theories of motion, heat, and other natural phenomena, it works pretty well in many situations. It fails miserably, though, in places that matter most, such as in setting public policy, where the collective intuitive decisions of individuals often result in harmful consequences for the public. We see this in decisions people make not getting vaccinated, driving while drunk, or expending energy without regard for greenhouse-gas emissions, and in many other science-related decisions as well.[13]

The lay public has always relied on this intuitive, gut-level, moral reasoning. Over one hundred and thirty years of formal science education hasn't changed that, despite targeting those very human tendencies toward irrationality. In fact, it's this continued reliance on intuitions rather than hard evidence that has resulted in the very problem we currently have with science education—it *seems* to make sense that doing science (the ultimate rational enterprise) will result in better thinking skills and that this eventually will give us the rational society we all hope for. It's too bad it's not that simple.[14]

What do we know at this point? We know that teaching science *content*, no matter how rigorously, does little to increase students' scientific reasoning abilities (which should be obvious). We also know that few teachers take the time to teach scientific reasoning or engage students in inquiry-based activities (and have few if any curricular materials to rely on). We also know that, even if they did (and did it well), students rarely come away with improved scientific reasoning skills as a result. This is because scientific thinking is really hard. It goes against the natural inclinations of everyday human cognition. One might wonder at this point, what's left? Why do we teach science at all? The problem lies with the science education we have—one narrowly focused on content mastery and, when addressed at all, on the internal workings of the scientific process. What we currently have is far too limited in scope to do the job we'd like to see done. It isn't that science education can't accomplish important general-education goals for the majority of American students. It's that to accomplish the most important goals, we need a much different kind of science education than what we've grown accustomed to.[15]

PART 3

WHAT WE NEED

CHAPTER 7

SCIENCE EDUCATION FOR BUILDING PUBLIC TRUST

Science education has been guided for too long by a loose set of assumptions about what it offers of value to the general public. I've tried to show in Part 2 the mismatch between the goals we talk about as a society (and have talked about for well over a hundred years) and what our schools realistically might be able to accomplish. By examining who makes up the population of high school students (in terms of likely higher education and career outcomes) and what lived experience and systematic research shows about how science intersects with daily life, I hope to push us to reconsider what we do in science classrooms and to what end.

It should be clear by this point that not all of the long-stated goals of science education are worth pursuing. The hard focus on preparing students for science-related jobs in the hopes of driving national economic growth (the national utilitarian argument), for example, does a disservice to the overwhelming majority of students who are neither in the technical-training pipeline nor interested in being swept into it. The content-centric curriculum that has come along with this goal (the default approach to science education), as we've seen, has done little to help realize the other, oft-repeated goals of personal utility, democratic decision-making, and better everyday thinking. Given this, we need to ask ourselves why we persist in teaching science the way we do when it's so clearly failing us.

Some might read this book so far as an argument against science education. However, nothing could be further from the truth. The argument is against an *unreflective* science education, one that doesn't meet our need for a healthy, productive public relationship with science in this country, the United States. Although some of the arguments for teaching science are, in light of what we know, no longer worth pursuing at the elementary and secondary school levels, others most surely are. But which ones?

To know where to focus, we should consider where the greatest need lies. Looking around us today, the most significant threat we face in society is to the collective use of intelligence to manage pressing science-related problems—problems that have the potential to overwhelm us all. Science, without question, is the foundation of that intelligence. It enables us to foresee and understand the consequences of our actions in the world and to develop new techniques that can be used to solve the myriad problems we encounter. But it does us little good if we ignore it—if we dismiss the knowledge it produces due to ignorance, political partisanship, or the cynical pursuit of power and wealth. The path to recognizing and realizing the social value of science, to mending the growing dysfunctional relationship between science and the public requires a better public understanding of both science—as a means of producing reliable knowledge—and the place of science in American society. In terms of the goals of science education, this might be thought of as a new goal entirely, one that I'll call *building public trust in science.* The central issue to be addressed with this is the problem of expertise.

* * *

We live in an incredibly complex world—socially, politically, economically, technologically, the list goes on. Almost every policy document on science education written since the 1930s has led with some acknowledgment of the knotty science-related issues society needs to grapple with. The opening paragraph of the NRC's *Framework for K-12 Science Education*, the blueprint for the Next Generation Science Standards, for example, explains most recently that "many of the challenges that face humanity now and in the future—related, for example, to the environment, energy, and health—require social, political, and economic solutions that must be informed deeply by knowledge of the underlying science and engineering."[1] These challenges aren't merely hypothetical. Over the past few years as a society, we have experienced the real effects of a global pandemic, climate change, severe weather events, contaminated drinking water, among many, many others. And the need for scientific knowledge to help us navigate these challenges has been starkly evident. What's necessary in every one of these instances, however, isn't for *all* of us to know the relevant science or some rudimentary summary of it, but rather to know who knows it best. That is, what science-related social issues always and necessarily call for is the judicious use of expertise.

Scientific expertise is an inescapable fact of modern life. Our limited individual understanding of the natural world requires us to rely on it to make the best, most intelligent decisions about the science-related issues we increasingly confront. Central to that reliance—to our relationship with science—is the matter of trust. As individuals, we have no independent means of judging the credibility of scientific knowledge. Various scholars over the years have written about trust being an irreducible element of science, of all knowledge in fact. And yet all around us, larger social forces have been working to slowly erode our trust in science, to whip up suspicion of the role of expertise in modern life. Unfortunately, the science education enterprise of late has turned a blind eye to this trend. It has continued to operate under the mistaken assumption that if only we learn more science content or master the essential elements of scientific practice or reasoning, we will have the tools necessary to resolve the problems we face. This isn't nearly enough though. As I explained earlier, the public rationality project—in which citizens are taught scientific thinking skills in the hope that they can be applied to current social problems—is more or less a dead end.[2]

What's needed instead is a renewed effort to bolster the cultural authority of scientific experts (or at the very least limit its further erosion). To accomplish this, we need a science education that acknowledges the central role of trust in the science–society relationship. Trusting that there are individuals who know more about how parts of the world work than the average person is essential for productively living with expertise in modern society. It's the only way we can truly realize all the benefits science has to offer, benefits that are the very reason society has placed such a high value on science education in the first place.

The closest thing we have had to a program of science education that frankly acknowledged the accommodation of scientific expertise as the central issue was that developed within the Harvard general-education program led by James Conant after World

War II. "We live in an age of experts," Conant explained in 1952. "As a consequence, one of our many problems is how to provide a basis for appraising the expert and his advice." How might science education accomplish this? he asked. Not by training more experts. But instead by helping students become "experts in judging experts." And a key learning outcome of this postwar general-education approach, as discussed in Chapter 1, was helping students see and understand the unique culture of the scientific community so that they might appreciate the nature of the research enterprise and understand the conditions necessary for its success. Conant sought to accomplish this through the use of historical case studies. Others in the Harvard program employed more contextual approaches, exploring with students the nature of scientific work and its interrelationship with society over time.[3]

However, the danger in this form of science education—one not fully appreciated by the postwar general-education reformers—was building in too much deference to expert authority. With deference comes the potential for abuse. This is the fundamental problem with systems that concentrate power in institutions or people who are unaccountable to the broader public. It provides the conditions for the free play of incompetence, corruption, and self-interest—for the exercise of authority that is less than transparently in the *public* interest. This was the situation in the late 1960s and early 1970s when concerns over environmental pollution and military escalation during the war in Vietnam seemed to point to a scientific enterprise more in thrall to defense-industry and corporate interests than to the greater good of society. The result wasn't a failure of *science* but rather a failure of individuals and institutions—a failure, in the end, of public supervision and systems of accountability. The result was a public pushback against science—a check on the experts that manifested in more government oversight, regulation, and cutbacks in funding—that seemed to be an attack on science itself. And for many, it was.[4]

The attacks ramped up from all sides throughout the second half of the twentieth century. Corporate hands in the tobacco and oil industries chipped away at the legitimacy of science by injecting doubt (exploiting public misunderstandings of science) into research on the cancer-causing effects of smoking and the impact of greenhouse gases on the climate. The religious right fought efforts of biologists to reintroduce evolutionary theory into the curriculum in the 1960s, claiming it undermined faith and didn't conform to the norms of proper scientific practice. In the academy, an emerging group of sociologists and philosophers began questioning the objectivity of science, suggesting that scientific truths were determined less by nature itself than by the culture, politics, and the professional interests of the scientists, setting off what became known as the "science wars" in the 1990s. More recently (and more dangerously), public skepticism of science has been wielded politically to disastrous effect. The casual dismissal of scientific expertise with respect to social distancing, mask-wearing, and vaccination among the right, for example, has resulted in the incalculable loss of life during the worldwide coronavirus pandemic to say nothing about the dire, long-term threats posed by unmitigated climate change.[5]

The efforts to rein in scientific authority that began in the 1950s and 1960s have risen into a tidal wave of outright public defiance that has moved the United States to the brink of instability. Respect for expertise needs to be rebuilt. However, if we've learned anything from the past, it's that we must balance public respect with a true sense of public control and agency. This is the needle we have to thread. We need a science education that promotes public recognition and appreciation of the specialized knowledge science has to offer and, at the same time, advances greater understanding of the proper role of science in society—the idea that science isn't something alien, to be feared or blindly obeyed, but is instead an enterprise that is an integral part of society, an extension of the public that can be used to improve the world we live in, to improve all of our lives.

What might this look like? In the realm of democratic decision-making, it would mean a clear seat for scientific expertise at the table as part of the process of grappling with science-related social issues. It would not mean having experts *make* decisions. Their role would be to identify the parameters of the issue in question and indicate the range of possible consequences for any particular course of action or policy decision. In other words, when people, as both citizens and political leaders, need information to make a decision, they would include relevant experts among the social networks and preferred information sources they rely on to help make that decision. As we've seen from the research on this topic, this is how such decisions are made, after all, in real-world practice.

Such an arrangement would not cede political decision-making power to the experts. Unchecked scientific authority wielded by a technocratic elite would only ensure continued injustice and social harm. Too many times have we seen the horrible oppression, marginalization, and mistreatment of certain racial and ethnic groups; the exploitation of natural resources by corporate interests; the manipulation of information to secure greater political power; among many examples that have resulted from the misuse of scientific authority. Sound decision-making requires, though, a fair hearing from those experts most knowledgeable (as deemed by professional credentials as well as lived experience) about the issues in question. It would mean, for example, weighing seriously the consensus reports of the Intergovernmental Panel on Climate Change, the testimony and guidance of epidemiologists during a pandemic, the input of geologists and physicists when considering the siting of a nuclear-waste facility, and so on. The decisions we make as a society would be our own (and might not even be the same as those some experts would make), but they would be made knowing—as much as is humanly possible—what the short- and long-term effects of those decisions would be.[6]

For the everyday matters of the average citizen, it would mean talking with their doctor or other medical professionals before deciding about their or their children's health care. It would mean being sure to locate and consult legitimate sources of information in libraries or online before deciding how they might vote, for example, on some statewide referendum related to energy policy. It would mean that people would recognize that not all information and sources of information (including friends, family members, and other individuals in their social network) are created equal—that some information is a better, more reliable guide for our actions than others.

The optimal relationship between science and the public, however, would need to involve more than just the open and transparent consideration of knowledge flowing one way from expert to policymaker or from scientist to citizen. It would require the ongoing direction and oversight of the research enterprise itself. Ideally, the public—through its elected representatives and other means both direct and indirect—would be more involved in determining research priorities, allocating governmental resources,

regulating research endeavors, shaping research-training programs, and other such things that constitute the scientific enterprise. This is the key, often overlooked part of the science–society
relationship—recognizing that the public has a legitimate say
over what and how science gets done.[7]

Of course, many would argue that the public already exerts its
influence in all of these areas through the various mechanisms
of federal appropriations, programs, and oversight. And although
this may be true in some nominal sense, it's clear that few members of the lay public *feel* this to be true in a real sense. A sense of
profound public alienation from science and its research endeavors seems closer to the lived experience of the average citizen. The
fact that the National Science Board in its *Science and Engineering
Indicators* treats public attitudes toward science as something to be
monitored and managed suggests that a true partnership has yet
to be realized.[8]

To change the current relationship between science and the
public from one of dependence and suspicion—the scientific
enterprise's dependence on public support and the public's dependence on scientific expertise (with suspicion on both sides)—to
one of mutual support and collaboration requires science education designed to rebuild public trust. This requires working to
improve the public understanding of science. The goal, however,
is not just for people to understand the insular social and intellectual practices of the scientific research community à la Conant
and his like-minded postwar education reformers. It has to extend
outward, to include the appreciation and acceptance of the place
of science in our broader culture (Conant sought this too to be
fair, but on his, more narrow terms).

By this I mean a recognition that science as an enterprise exists
as an extension of our humanity, that it operates not as an entity

unto itself, isolated and aloof (though it's often perceived as such) but rather as an extension of our greater community. We need to see science as the part of society that helps us realize our shared goals, and we should all expect to have a say in what kind of research gets done and how it gets done to ensure that it will provide the greatest benefits for the greatest number of us.[9]

* * *

How might science classrooms change if they were to focus on building trust as a means of fostering more effective democratic decision-making? Most immediately, they would abandon the almost singular focus on disciplinary content knowledge. As we've seen, that approach gets us to none of the key goals to which science education aspires. The emphasis rather should be twofold—first, on teaching students the way that science arrives at knowledge about the world (this is what philosophers sometimes refer to as the epistemology of science); and, second, on teaching students about the role of science in society, that is, how science functions as an institution in our modern world.

Teaching How Scientists Know What They Know

The first of these two emphases—teaching how science produces knowledge—should ideally target authentic instances of scientific research and practice as much as possible. For instance, instead of having students learn that atoms are made up of protons, neutrons, and electrons and that those subatomic particles themselves are built from even smaller particles (such as quarks and leptons), they would explore *how* physicists came to know this. What did they do and see at various times in history to arrive at the understanding they have today? What equipment did they use to generate their data?—think cathode-ray discharge tubes, pieces of gold foil, and bubble and cloud chambers. What tentative theories did they explore that were later revised in light of new ideas and evidence?

Exploring the process of knowledge construction in this way can't be done following the steps of some scripted laboratory exercise to verify what we already know. It might involve using historical case studies similar to those Conant and others used at Harvard, newly developed text material describing episodes of knowledge construction, multimedia presentations, or dramatic re-enactments. It might include learning about current research projects with guest-speaking appearances by scientists themselves to explain their work. There might even be some simulated laboratory activities to demonstrate how relevant data are generated, processed, and analyzed—always keeping in mind the larger goal of seeing what it is scientists are seeking to understand and how they know when they've reached that understanding, when they've attained knowledge about some corner of the world that can be relied upon and used.

More important for the larger purpose of public understanding would be to expose students to the *variety* of research that scientists engage in. Too often, school science teaches that the process of science (when it's dealt with at all) entails experimentation, specifically experimentation involving the control of variables strategy, an approach wherein all the variables in an experiment are held constant except one—the variable scientists are testing for an effect. This is, in fact, the only strategy asked about in the *Science and Engineering Indicators* assessment of public understanding of the scientific process. And it's the one that science-education researchers and cognitive psychologists continually emphasize in their work on teaching scientific reasoning. Science, however, involves far more epistemological variety than this.[10]

Scientists do so much more than conduct experiments. In addition to experimentation, scientists engage in historical analysis when they seek to understand sequences of past events, such as when they ponder the origins of the Universe (Did everything begin with the Big Bang? What were the stages in the development of our galaxy?) or the patterns of organic evolution over time (At what point did the human species diverge from other primates?) or the history of the Earth's changing climate (When and how long were the various ice ages?). This work relies on indirect evidence and the consideration of a wide range of disparate observations that scientists bring together to build chronologies of the past in much the same way police detectives piece together what happened at a crime scene.[11]

Other non-experimental scientific work includes exploring natural processes that occur so slowly that they are beyond the capacity of direct human observation. Examples here include geologic change on Earth and other planets (extremely slow-moving tectonic plates and the gradual formation of canyons by water erosion), macroevolutionary speciation (the evolution of birds from dinosaurs), and the formation of stars. Climate change is similarly an incredibly complex phenomenon that has occurred on a much longer time scale that scientists have studied using both historical and current climate data along with computer modeling techniques to project likely future conditions. Unlike in fields of atomic physics and chemistry, these systems can't be manipulated in real time to test the ideas scientists come up with. No simple experiment can be done to prove the truth of any particular scientific claim definitively.[12]

Extending the curriculum beyond its narrow focus on the experimental sciences is an essential step for fostering greater public trust. Science isn't a single thing but rather a description of a variety of research practices that examine a wide range of phenomena, each of which requires different methods, background assumptions, and techniques to effectively make sense of. The public is often quick to dismiss the contributions of scientific research that differs from the more familiar experimental sciences they learned about in school and that we often see in the media. Statements like "you can't *prove* that global warming isn't just the result of a natural cycle" and "no one has ever actually *seen* a new species evolve" provide plenty of evidence of widespread public misunderstanding of how science functions in all its diversity.[13]

Teaching—in painstaking detail—how scientists come to know what they know is an essential step in rebuilding public trust. It's far too easy for skeptics to wave away established scientific findings when they think it's simply some group's pet theory or speculative suggestion. However, in seeing what has gone into building the knowledge we have of the world and how scientists go about making sense of the natural events happening around us, it's hoped that students and the public would begin to appreciate the legitimacy of the expertise scientists possess in their various fields. This would allow them to see scientists as individuals who can be relied on when difficult personal or civic questions need to be answered. Building reliable knowledge is difficult; it takes time and effort. This needs to be fully recognized.

Teaching about the Scientific Enterprise in Society

Teaching about the epistemological context just described—*how* we know what we know about the world rather than just *what* we know—is one key element of the science education we need. Yet, it isn't enough, nor is it completely new. Others have called for greater attention to this aspect of science in the past. Educators have tried to build this approach into science classrooms, going as far back as Conant's work at Harvard in the 1940s. This, however, is only the first part of what I would propose. The second emphasis in this vision for science education would go beyond the epistemological to include the social and institutional elements of the scientific enterprise—things that few if any high school or college science courses ever explore.[14]

For the public to begin to see science as an essential part of the larger culture, we need to help students understand the social elements of scientific work, both in the construction of knowledge and in how it is supported and functions in society. This means teaching about argumentation, peer review, and consensus formation; it means teaching that science isn't simply an exercise in logic in which the data, once collected, lead unequivocally toward some obvious conclusion. Data and observations never speak for themselves; they always require scientists to interpret them. Students need to experience and realize that learning about the world is an inherently social process that requires debate and negotiation and is far from straightforward and that the scientific knowledge produced, tentative though it may be, is nonetheless tested and durable enough to act on.

A step beyond this entails delving into questions about the institutional operations of science. Here is where the path diverges significantly from traditional instruction. Science classes should include explorations of how research priorities are determined, who decides on funding allocations, how funding sources influence the nature of the research that's done (for good and for ill), the ways scientific research is regulated in various fields, how human subjects are protected, who does science and what it takes to enter the profession, and which institutions and agencies are representative of the scientific consensus and are, therefore, trustworthy.[15]

Students might learn, for example, about how AIDS activists mobilized to pressure the National Institutes of Health to revise its guidelines for clinical studies and drug approval in the interest of patients in the 1970s and 1980s or the early development of the Superconducting Super Collider in Texas and the eventual decision of Congress to scrap the project in the 1990s. They might explore the debate over federal funding of stem-cell research in the late 1990s and early 2000s or, most recently, about the public–private partnerships involved in developing the COVID-19 vaccine. They might learn about the Centers for Disease Control and its public mission and responsibilities, what the role of the National Academy of Sciences is in advising the government, and about the organization and structure of the Intergovernmental Panel on Climate Change (IPCC).

At the other, darker end of the spectrum, they might explore organizations that have historically sought to undermine science or misrepresent the scientific consensus for their own self-interest. As with the strictly epistemological lessons, teachers could employ rich case studies, historical narratives, and guest speakers providing first-hand accounts to illustrate and bring to life the nuts and bolts of how various institutions have functioned to mediate or manipulate the relationship between scientific expertise and the public. Case studies might include the evolution/creation debate in the United States, where groups like the Institute for Creation Research have advanced religious creation stories dressed up as legitimate science (such as creation science and intelligent design), the history of tobacco industry efforts to exploit public misunderstanding of science to raise doubts about the connection between smoking and cancer, and the public debates over human-induced climate change. Students could even spend time tracking the way science is represented and misrepresented in mass media and social media for partisan, commercial, personal, or sensationalist objectives in any variety of other one-off instances.[16]

* * *

To achieve these goals, one could imagine a science course or even a whole curriculum organized by topics instead of by the traditional subjects of biology, chemistry, and physics. Such topics might include:

• How science learns about the natural world: the experimental sciences, the historical sciences, modeling and prediction;
• The social structure of scientific communities and the importance of consensus in knowledge production;
• Where to find reliable knowledge for personal and public purposes;
• The public role in the scientific enterprise: research agendas, funding, and regulation; and
• Science and culture.

Such courses could productively engage social studies teachers who might work alongside or in parallel with science teachers. It might bring in teachers of communication arts or media studies who could help students develop more sophisticated media literacy skills as students try to negotiate a world in which everyone feels entitled to their own set of facts. Many of the units would undoubtedly include deep dives into traditional disciplinary topics such as electricity and magnetism, Darwinian evolution, and the kinetic-molecular theory. And students would certainly learn a wide range of scientific facts in the process. The primary purpose, though, would be to provide students with larger understandings of the scientific enterprise rather than isolated technical knowledge.[17]

The instructional focus outlined above would provide students with both the epistemological foundations (how scientists know things) and the institutional context (where science fits in modern society) necessary for rebuilding the relationship—and trust—between science and the public. A shift in emphasis of this sort would be akin to teaching "American political systems" instead of "US history" in social studies. One might think students can infer how our governmental institutions work by studying the events of our country's pasts. However, they would likely learn far more by examining those institutions directly and how they function as mechanisms of government, in both theory and practice. Why aren't there analogous courses in the science curriculum that engage students in what, where, and how science gets done?

A shift in science teaching of this sort would also provide a more natural space for the currently neglected culture goal. Much of what is taught in our high schools aims to foster cultural appreciation among students. We teach art, music, foreign languages, English literature, and history to help students understand who they are and where they fit in the scope of human existence. Such courses promote a greater understanding of the self and others. They create social cohesion and highlight what humanity is capable of, both good and bad. Why shouldn't science be taught with similar purposes in mind?

Students should have the opportunity to explore the transcendent cultural questions that advocates like Gerald Holton and Carl Sagan have posed, questions that would help us begin to see, in Sagan's words, "how we achieved our present understanding of the cosmos, how the cosmos has shaped our evolution and our culture, and what our fate may be."[18] Exploring these in a meaningful way in schools is essential for bridging the science–public divide. Looking at the recurring interactions between science and the public socially, economically, intellectually, and culturally would promote the productive integration of science into our everyday world.

One final, key benefit to this approach in terms of building public trust is its potential for diversifying the country's science and technology workforce. We know that women and people of color (African Americans, American Indians and Alaska Natives, Hispanics, Native Hawaiians and other Pacific Islanders) have been underrepresented in science, technology, and biomedical fields for far too long. Although women make up over half the US population, they earn proportionally fewer undergraduate and graduate degrees in nearly all the typical natural-science majors. The same is true for African American and Hispanic/Latinx students whose share of science-degrees-earned falls significantly short of their general prevalence in the population. The numbers get progressively even less representative looking at the share of women and people of color in scientific and technical occupations, in tenured faculty positions at four-year colleges and universities, and among physicians and physician-scientists.[19]

"But why should we be concerned with increasing diversity in the sciences?" you might ask. "Haven't you just spent seven chapters saying that science education should be moving away from its current emphasis on career preparation, away from its obsessive focus on filling the STEM pipeline?" I have. Let me explain.

We know that there are high levels of scientific and medical mistrust among women and people of color in the US. There are numerous reasons for this. There are well-known historical instances of abuse, from the infamous cases of the medical appropriation of cell lines from Henrietta Lacks to the Tuskegee syphilis study in which white researchers allowed infected African-American subjects to go untreated to study the course of the disease over decades during the twentieth century. In addition, there are the less dramatic practices of the repeated exclusion of female subjects from drug-testing clinical trials to the everyday disparities in patterns of pain management and other disease treatments resulting from systemic racism and implicit bias among physicians and other healthcare workers.[20]

When people from marginalized groups look at those in the scientific, technical, and medical professions, they don't see themselves. They see a population that reflects the dominant, privileged culture of America. That difference between whom they see in power—offering advice, policy recommendations, and expertise—and whom they see in their own families and neighborhoods breeds feelings of distrust, feelings that have been validated by the repeated instances of historical mistreatment and neglect.

A minimum requirement for addressing that difference and remedying the ongoing injustices being perpetrated is precisely to recruit, educate, and mentor underrepresented populations into these fields so that our scientific and technical institutions look like the public they serve. Having more women and people of color in these professions will make it more likely that their voices, concerns, and challenges will be heard and taken seriously. It will ensure that they're part of setting the research agendas, conducting the peer review, advising government agencies, and communicating with the public. The needs and problems of women, Blacks, Hispanics, Native Americans, and other marginalized groups would begin to be addressed in meaningful ways. The more diversity we have in science, the more responsive science will be to the broader public. The more responsive it is, the more likely the public—all the public—will invest its trust in science.[21]

Intensifying current science education practices or expanding AP course offerings to more students in the hope that we increase the number of women and people of color in science majors, however, isn't the answer. Diversifying the STEM pipeline requires a different kind of science education—one that's not focused on the traditional model of technical training, at least not in our secondary schools. The content-focused approach that has predominated at all levels has, in fact, long been used as a tool to weed out students not viewed as having the necessary drive or natural talent to succeed in rigorous science majors. In sociologist Elaine Seymour's well-known study *Talking about Leaving* and its follow-up publication *Talking about Leaving Revisited*, researchers documented that one of the critical factors responsible for students switching out of STEM majors was introductory science teaching that covered too much material at too rapid a pace. The all too familiar approach consists of the superficial coverage of scientific facts and concepts with little effort to foster deeper understanding. Among the students most severely affected by this have been and continue to be women and students of color.[22]

Turning away from the current emphasis on technical training and toward teaching science in a way that opens up space for building understanding and trust in science and scientific institutions is not only good for society generally but, perhaps counterintuitively, has the potential to draw *more* women and students of color into the science-training pipeline. Rather than setting these students up to identify themselves as "science" people or "non-science" people as traditional, content-focused approaches typically do (which often turns off more students than it turns on), a science classroom focused on how science works and functions in its social context is likely to provide a more welcoming environment for all students—not just the 7 percent. Increasing the diversity of those who make up the scientific enterprise in this country (if not the overall numbers) is essential for ensuring a long-term productive relationship between science and the public.[23]

* * *

Frankly, much of what I'm calling for is well beyond the scope of what we currently think of as science education. Teaching how scientists became convinced that the Earth's surface consists of moving plates is no real stretch from a traditional perspective. A little more historical narrative to go with the details of the current model of plate tectonics is all you need. Looking at the cultural consequences of Galileo's arguments for a Sun-centered solar system is more of a lift; but there are decent materials out there that teachers could certainly work from. Taking on questions about the public role in setting research priorities or how scientific institutions function in society, however, would be entirely new and exotic without question. Yet making all these things the focus of instruction is crucial if we hope to shift the public perception of science from being viewed as something *outside* of society and culture to being viewed as *an integral part of it*, as something that citizens themselves have a role in shaping as legislators, school board members, community leaders, and voters. With this, we can achieve a dual purpose—science education for culture's sake and for a kind of cultural appreciation that leads to more effective democratic participation.[24]

Yes, such topics lie outside the box of the science education we have—the content-centered approach currently found in most schools. But what sense does it make to continue down the rutted path we're on, to invest in a system that we *hope* will produce more scientists and engineers but has, in fact, created a society in which too many citizens routinely ignore the recommendations of the scientists and engineers we already have. This seems to be the very definition of counterproductive. Focusing instead on building public appreciation of science and how an understanding of its culture as a part of the broad and diverse culture all around us has much greater potential for producing a win–win situation— we foster a public that understands and is receptive to scientific expertise and, in the process, lay the groundwork for more students eventually to enter the science-training pipeline should they be interested in pursuing that route (and should they actually be needed).

CHAPTER 8

HOW TO GET THERE

From the first days that science education was added to the high school curriculum, there have been a host of claims made about why it's socially beneficial and worth the considerable emphasis and financial investment society has made and continues to make in its pursuit. The benefits, as we've seen, have included everything from moral uplift in the late nineteenth century to better thinking skills to innovation-driven economic prosperity. Yet, despite all of the benefits claimed for science education, we have rarely matched them with what we expect students to learn in their science classrooms. As a society, we've either assumed that good, high-quality science teaching was (and is) more or less capable of achieving all of these goals, or we've never really thought about it much at all. We seem to have just nodded approvingly at the presumed benefits while allowing classroom instruction to default to the content-focused, mind-numbing approach that all of us have experienced at one time or another, an approach determined by a combination of overstuffed textbooks and the disciplinary fields themselves, which became ever more entrenched with the rise of national standards and standardized assessments created in response to the economic crises that began in the 1970s.

It should be obvious that different social purposes require different kinds of science teaching, curricular emphases, and instructional methods. Think about it—a science curriculum geared toward preparing students for technical careers, of course, would look completely unlike one aimed at developing scientific reasoning skills, for instance (setting aside the fact that achieving a high level of scientific reasoning among the public is an unlikely outcome). However, we continue to go about our business teaching science with no real thought as to *how* it might accomplish what we just assume it accomplishes. It's essential that we connect all the dots, that we consider what the most desirable social goals of science education might be in light of what research tells us about how people learn and actually use science in their lives and design our science education accordingly.

So what do we know? We know that most people don't end up in science-related careers, nor is there some overwhelming demand for technically trained workers (hidden or in plain view) that is going unmet. We know that people mostly forget the science content knowledge they learn in school or, if they remember it, rarely use it to address everyday personal matters. Even less likely do they use science to make sense of the far more consequential challenges we face as a society. We also know that the fuzzy faith many have that doing science in a high school lab will somehow increase our capacity for rational thought and action is grossly misplaced. Everyday human cognition just doesn't appear to work that way. We know all of these things, and all of these things point to the sure failure of our current approach to science education.

To be clear, the logical conclusion from this isn't that we don't need science education. It is that we need a science education tailored to a worthwhile and achievable social purpose, one that takes all that we know into account. Building a sustainable, mutually supportive relationship between science and the public is the purpose we need to shoot for. There is without question a rising demand for a public that understands and trusts that scientific knowledge is a good thing and that it's something the public has a legitimate voice in shaping and directing. We need people to see science as an essential part of our common culture, an extension of ourselves that we can use to meet our needs and solve our problems, collectively and in all our diversity. The technical training-focused science education we currently have comes nowhere close to getting us to this goal.

Change won't be easy. History tells us that we're more likely to fail than succeed. Dozens of reforms have been initiated over the years only to fade away with little real effect.[1] The reasons for this are many. For one, the science teachers we have and prepare have themselves been thoroughly immersed in the content-based approach. For them, learning science is all about mastering disciplinary content and solving textbook problems. It's not surprising that they teach as they've been taught. Moreover, scientific facts and principles are simply easier to teach, and student learning of these facts is easier to assess than learning goals that center on students understanding how science is done or engaging in complex socioscientific reasoning. The available instructional materials and textbooks reinforce the focus on content (and a lot of it) too. There's also the enduring belief in the myth that a focus on science content (the more advanced the better) is the path for all students to better jobs, a highly trained technical workforce, and economic prosperity despite all the evidence to the contrary. It's the message we hear all around us every day. All these things work together to maintain the status quo.

Perhaps the greatest obstacle to change, however, is that the content-based approach serves its own purpose. The American architect Louis Sullivan famously said, "form ever follows function." And the rarely acknowledged function of the current system is all about political accountability and social mobility. A content-based science education proves to be one in which it's easy to assess students, which makes it easy to sort them. The increasing "rigor" of science courses, going from biology to chemistry to physics and math-based physics (as it's sometimes called) to the whole suite of Advanced Placement courses is all perfectly adapted to a credentials market, the idea that each subject or level passed shows up like a gold star on the student's transcript, with more stars unlocking access to the next higher tier of selective colleges or providing actual cash savings to parents in the form of AP credits secured via a suitable AP exam score.[2]

Such a system offers little more than that star or checkmark on a transcript. The ability of students to calculate the voltage drop across a capacitor, successfully balance a chemical equation, repeat the steps in the Krebs cycle from memory, or correctly mark an orbital-filling diagram has almost no value beyond what it demonstrates for the awarding of the credential—the passing of the course or the score on a standardized test. It results in a kind of blind science teaching, where the primary goal of every class is to do whatever is necessary to get the students to repeat back facts from the lectures and the textbook and to get correct answers to the problems in any given textbook problem set. Teachers teach and students learn all kinds of mnemonics, heuristics, and short-cuts designed to produce those correct answers. The entire system is reinforced by happy students (who feel a sense of accomplishment in the A or B they earned in the class and whose prospects for admission into the college of their choice has bumped up a notch), happy teachers (who feel as though they've done their job—the students got the answers right after all), happy parents (who don't have to pay for as many college credits and can take pride in their student's accomplishments), and happy school board members (who delight in the high student test scores that they can report to the community).

Yet none of this "learning" does anyone any real good, at least not any good that derives from the substance of what's learned. The historian of education David Labaree, some years back, distinguished between two forms of education, that which has *use value* and that which has *exchange value*. Things taught within a use-value framework, he explained, are valuable because the content of what's taught has intrinsic worth. That is, the knowledge itself provides a means for doing something. Things taught within an exchange-value framework, on the other hand, have worth only to the extent that they can be traded for something else. "The value of education from this point of view," he wrote, "is not intrinsic but extrinsic, because the primary aim is to exchange one's education for something more substantial": college admission, credits toward a degree, a job, or even elevated cultural status. What students currently learn in their science classes, as we've seen, has very little real use-value. The exchange-value framework, though, ensures that things are unlikely to change. This is the function that has served to maintain the form of science education we have today.[3]

In this book, I've offered a different vision of what science education might look like, one that would have students examine how knowledge is made and made differently from one discipline to the next. It would have students learn about where science sits as a knowledge-producing institution in society and the value scientific expertise offers. It would also let them in on the little-known secret that science is a tool to be used for whatever purposes the public wants to accomplish, not something to be guarded and controlled by a scientific elite operating in isolation from the rest of us.

This kind of science education, difficult as it might be to implement, has the "use value" we are looking for. It would move us toward restoring public trust and, eventually, living more intelligently in the world. Getting from where we are to where we need to be will require fundamental changes in several areas. I will admit there's no obvious path we can take, much less any set of prescriptive steps to follow to get there. Maybe this book is just the first step, which is starting the conversation about what school science education should really be about. In that spirit of conversation, there are three essential changes or shifts in thinking that would need to happen to get us to a science education that builds public trust. There are certainly more than these. Again, I offer these as a way to get the conversation started. I present them in no particular order.

Revitalize the Civic Mission of the High School

The history of American schooling shows us, if anything, that our educational systems have been established and maintained for a variety of purposes since their founding. The ability to serve multiple constituencies, in fact, is perhaps the primary reason for the remarkable success of public education in this country. The first high schools in the United States had a place both for the college-bound and for those seeking skills necessary to thrive in the growing commercial sector of the country during a period of rapid industrialization. High school prepared both the future bookkeeper and baccalaureate. Underlying all of this was the widespread commitment to the civic purpose of public schooling. Schools were the place where we prepared students to be citizens. Indeed, there has probably been no more powerful argument for public education in those early years than the need to unite a diverse country through a common educational experience. Schooling was the means to realize the *e pluribus unum* aspirations of America.[4]

Science's place in that story, naturally, has followed a similar script in terms of diversity of purposes, gaining a foothold in the nineteenth-century curriculum on the promise of its practical applications, shifting to its efficacy for mental training and moral improvement, then cycling through all the other arguments we've encountered over the years before landing on the current version of practical application—science education in the service of economic growth for national (and individual) prosperity. The democratic or civic goals of education in science and in education generally—in a substantive, meaningful sense—have gotten lost since the utilitarian turn that came after World War II.

That utilitarian turn, however, has taken us into a dead end. As we've seen, there's a mismatch between the educational and workforce paths the overwhelming majority of students are on and the kind of science education we are providing. There always has been. We've just been blinded by our assumption that technical training for all is the ticket to national prosperity. The science teaching we have has never done much for most high school students—other than turn them off to science and waste precious public resources for little real societal gain.

That said, we desperately need science education. We need a public that understands and appreciates how science works and what it can offer society along the lines I have discussed, and this understanding is precisely the outcome that high school is best suited to accomplish. It's the one place where students of all backgrounds and future destinations still come together as members of a community—as citizens. Science education in this context should be about fostering broad understandings of science that might secure a more productive relationship between science and the public. This is what we should want for *all* future citizens instead of a system that sorts and tracks students based on presumed educational and career destinations, a system that isolates students from one another as they grind along the traditional disciplinary subject pathways and leaves them in the end with almost nothing of value.

Given the acute challenges our democratic institutions have faced of late, it's not surprising that there has been a renewed focus on civic education in the United States. Both the Brookings Institution and the National Academy of Education have made high-profile calls for schools to refocus on teaching skills of citizenship and civic discourse. The challenges posed by science-related social issues, such as the ongoing coronavirus pandemic and climate crisis—two key issues identified by the National Academy of Education report on this topic—highlight the problem of "how we can, at multiple levels of society, strive to work together to address our collective needs." An education designed to meet those needs is essential. A science education that focuses on the civic goal of rebuilding public trust in science for all students will do just that.[5]

There are some who will continue to worry about the 7 percent of science-bound ninth graders I described in Chapter 3 or perhaps think that the somewhat radical change I've suggested will sacrifice too much essential science content knowledge to this "other" stuff—"How can we teach these new things and still cover what's in the textbook?" For one, students would learn more than enough science content in the course of examining how scientists developed the central concepts and theories in their respective disciplines. Exploring how we came to believe in atoms and the particles that make them up will result, naturally, in students grasping the essential ideas about atomic theory. The same would be true for Darwin's work on evolution by natural selection and Wegener's theory of continental drift, among the many examples that could be cited. A particularly beneficial side effect would be students coming away with a far richer and enduring conceptual understanding of that material than they would have obtained if they followed the traditional forced march through the textbook, understanding that is essential for any sort of advanced technical training.

Moreover, shifting the secondary school science curriculum toward building public trust for democratic participation would in no way undermine existing avenues of technical preparation. It would leave programs at two-year colleges, tech schools, and the undergraduate and graduate majors in science at colleges and universities fully intact, free to do what they've always done. It makes far more sense, I would argue, to think about the various institutions that make up our educational system as having differentiated roles given the different audiences each serves.

When we think about our high schools and middle schools, we should be thinking about the ninety-plus percentage of students who have no interest or need for technical training in science, who need—desperately—a better understanding of what science is, how it works, and how it can serve our larger social needs. And learning outcomes such as these, I would emphasize, are just as valuable for those students planning to go on to science careers as they are for everyone else. Let's allow secondary schools to concentrate on general education goals and leave the advanced training to institutions and programs designed for that purpose (and for that smaller group of students).

Some of you will still want to hold out. "Maybe this new approach makes sense for the majority of students," you say. "But let's at least keep a track for those students who *really are* interested in going into the sciences." It would, after all, only be for that 7 percent. But, of course, history and human nature tell us how that would end up. The future-scientist track would be seen as the more "rigorous," a track for the "serious" students. It would inevitably default to the college-bound pathway (and gradually expand accordingly), with the science-for-general-education courses being reserved for those deemed not quite as "capable" as their science-track peers. The general-ed track would be useful, naturally, and important for teaching citizenship skills to those "general" students, as if the college-bound students needn't bother themselves with such "ordinary" concerns.

This isn't the science education we need. Indeed, such an arrangement would only further erode public trust in science and contribute to the continuing dysfunctional relationship we already have between science and the public. The future of our democratic culture and system of government requires nothing less than abandoning the old ways and embracing an entirely new approach—for everyone.

Change the Way We Prepare Science Teachers

It's perhaps easy to say that science teaching should move away from its focus on content knowledge to emphasize teaching instead how scientists arrived at that knowledge, how science and the broader culture have mutually influenced one other, and the institutional aspects of the scientific enterprise (including peer review, funding, regulation, training, and so on) without acknowledging that it requires teachers who know about all these things in order to teach them.

We know that the vast majority of science teachers are fundamentally unprepared for this dramatically different vision, and this is primarily because policymakers, school board members, teacher education professionals, and the public have assumed that disciplinary knowledge—that is, knowing the facts, theories, and techniques of science—is the key to high-quality teaching. Many believe that as long as teachers understand and can explain to students how to calculate allele frequencies or set up and run a titration experiment or draw a free-body diagram, then they're good to go. Knowledge of the field is first and foremost. For this reason, the gold standard for highly qualified teachers has long been having an undergraduate major in the subject they're teaching.[6]

Teacher certification and licensure programs in secondary science across the United States have been built on this assumption. Students seeking to enter the profession typically earn their teaching license in one of three ways. Many do so through an undergraduate teacher education program in which they earn credits in science courses that add up to a major in one of the disciplines, take a set number of education courses (in teaching methods, educational foundations, and educational psychology, for example), and complete a supervised student-teaching experience. Others enter post-baccalaureate or master's degree programs in education having previously earned an undergraduate degree in one or more of the sciences or are certified through an alternative pathway such as those offered by Teach for America or The New Teacher Project, where candidates complete their education coursework during their initial years of full-time teaching. The core requirement across all these pathways is science subject-matter competence, demonstrated through coursework or, less commonly, with a passing score on a standardized subject-matter test. It's no wonder that the students in my methods class came up with the textbook table-of-contents lists they did for their course outlines. That's all they've ever learned.[7]

In order to create science classrooms that foster public trust in science, teachers need to know more than this. They need to learn about the epistemologies and practices of the different research fields. They need to know the process and path of knowledge production. And they must study the institutions of science and how they operate, are funded, and are regulated. Preparation for this kind of teaching would require prospective teachers to take a wider range of science subjects in college alongside courses in the history, philosophy, and sociology of science. There is also a need for courses on public engagement with science, science communication, and the politics of expertise—courses that examine how individuals and deliberative bodies engage with science and make decisions about matters that affect our lives. Options like these currently exist mainly at the graduate level and typically at larger research universities—and often only those with science-and-technology studies programs or centers. Creating undergraduate versions of these graduate courses for future science teachers—or any interested undergrad—would go a long way to move science education in the right direction.

All this is to say that science teacher education programs need to look very different from how they do currently. Future science teachers need a much broader education than the state officials who set teacher certification requirements have been willing to settle for. The recent trend toward more alternative certification programs that seek to bring career changers from fields such as engineering into teaching (to alleviate teacher shortages brought about by public underfunding of education) makes it even less likely for us to enact the changes we need. We're clearly going in the wrong direction. In those programs, as long as candidates possess the requisite undergraduate science major or its equivalent, they are fast-tracked into the classroom. Yet, as we've seen, bare-minimum levels of content mastery won't get the job done. If those going into teaching only ever learn science as technical content, students in the nation's schools can never hope to understand science in a way that builds the trust necessary to realize a mutually beneficial relationship between science and the public.[8]

Build a Science Education Based on Evidence

The foundation of science is its commitment to the evidence of our senses, that the hypotheses, theories, and conjectures scientists come up with are all eventually tested by comparing them to what happens in the world. However, we continue to allow a whole series of untested working hypotheses guide students' experiences in science classrooms across the country.

- We assume that learning the scientific accounts and explanations of various aspects of the world—of phase changes, heat transfer, species variability, or human immune response—will enable us to make better everyday decisions.
- We imagine that engaging in the process of science—doing labs, collecting water samples, or measuring daily temperature and humidity—will help us think critically and reason logically in our day-to-day affairs.
- We accept—even double down on—the belief that raising standardized test scores and increasing Advanced Placement enrollments will spur technological innovation and lead to national economic prosperity.
- And we feel in our hearts that those higher science test scores and the repeated immersion in science laboratories will somehow translate into a public willing and able to intelligently debate and come to enlightened policy decisions about some of the most challenging science-related challenges of our time.

Yet, the problem remains that we have no hard evidence to support any of these assumptions or working hypotheses about science education—certainly not for the science education we currently have or even that the latest policy initiatives aspire to. It seems beyond comprehension that the overwhelming majority of scientists and science educators continue to maintain their commitments to these faith-based positions without seeking evidence that would support or refute them. It seems that the intuitive theories about the benefits of science teaching so many of us possess are incredibly powerful indeed.

In the preceding pages, I've tried to point out the flaws in these assumptions. There is plenty of evidence to draw on from a variety of sources, including the fields of developmental psychology, science communication, cultural cognition, economics, sociology, history, and corners of science education. And we have data from agencies such as the Census Bureau, the Bureau of Labor Statistics, and the National Center for Education Statistics, and even from our own experience—if we stop to reflect on it—to help us see the situation before us. We only need to use this knowledge of how education works, how people make sense of the world around them, and how they interact with others individually and collectively to create the kind of science education we desperately need.

If there's only one thing readers take away from this book, it should be the message that what we're currently doing isn't working, that it simply cannot work given what we know about how we live with and use science in our lives. There is plenty of evidence, in fact, that what we're currently doing is making things worse, that what we're doing, while seeming to meet pressing societal needs, is actually making it harder for science to grow and thrive as an essential part of our culture. What I've laid out in these pages is a reason to change, a reason to do something different from what we've been doing for the past sixty years or so. My only hope is that we begin to really think about why it is we think science education is so important to our future and work to create a science education that will realize that vision—that is, to think about why it is we teach science, and why we should.

NOTES

Introduction

1 National Science Board, "Science and Technology: Public Attitudes, Knowledge, and Interest," in *Science and Engineering Indicators 2020* (Alexandria, VA: National Science Foundation, 2020).

2 Andrew Jewett, *Science under Fire: Challenges to Scientific Authority in Modern America* (Cambridge, MA: Harvard University Press, 2020); Kim Tolley, "School Vaccination Wars: The Rise of Anti-Science in the American Anti-Vaccination Societies, 1879-1929," *History of Education Quarterly* 59 (2019): 161–194.

3 Edward J. Larson, *Trial and Error: The American Controversy over Creation and Evolution*, 3rd edn. (New York: Oxford University Press, 2003); Sopan Deb, "Kyrie Irving Doesn't Know if the Earth Is Round or Flat. He Does Want to Discuss It," *New York Times,* June 8, 2018; Yasmeen Abutaleb, Ashley Parker, Josh Dawsey, and Philiip Rucker, "The Inside Story of How Trump's Denial, Mismanagement and Magical Thinking Led to the Pandemic's Dark Winter," *Washington Post,* December 19, 2020.

4 While "science literacy" is the grammatically correct phrasing of this concept, "scientific literacy" is more commonly used. For that reason, I use it throughout the book.

5 Drew Desilver, "U.S. Students' Academic Achievement Still Lags that of Their Peers in Many Other Countries," Pew Research Center, February 15, 2017. Retrieved June 18, 2021 from https://www.pew research.org/fact-tank/2017/02/15/u-s-students-internationally-math -science/; Emily Richmond, "How Do American Students Compare to Their International Peers?" *Atlantic Monthly* (December 2016); Lauren Camera, "NAEP Shows Little to No Gains in Math, Reading for U.S. Students," *US News and World Report,* April 10, 2018; National Science Board, *Science and Engineering Indicators 2018* (Alexandria, VA: National Science Foundation, 2018).

6 American COMPETES Act, Public Law 110-69, 121 Stat. 572 (2007), sec. 6121; American Association for the Advancement of Science (AAAS), *Science for All Americans: Project 2061* (Washington, DC: American Association for the Advancement of Science, 1989); AAAS, *Benchmarks for Science Literacy* (New York: Oxford University Press, 1994); National Research Council, *National Science Education Standards* (Washington, DC: National Academy Press, 1996); National Research Council, *A Framework for K–12 Science Education: Practices, Crosscutting Concepts, and Core Ideas* (Washington, DC: National Academies Press, 2012); see also NGSS Lead States, *Next Generation Science Standards: For States, by States* (Washington, DC: National Academies Press, 2013).

7 John L. Rudolph, *Scientists in the Classroom: The Cold War Reconstruction of American Science Education* (New York: Palgrave, 2002), and John L. Rudolph, *How We Teach Science: What's Changed, and Why It Matters* (Cambridge, MA: Harvard University Press, 2019); George E. DeBoer, *A History of Ideas in Science Teaching: Implications for Practice* (New York: Teachers College Press, 1991).

Chapter 1

1 *Cosmos*, episode 1, "The Shores of the Cosmic Ocean," directed by Adrian Malone, written by Carl Sagan, Ann Druyan, and Steven Soter, featuring Carl Sagan, aired September 28, 1980, on PBS.

2 *Cosmos*, "The Shores of the Cosmic Ocean"; Dave Itzkoff, "'Family Guy' Creator Part of 'Cosmos' Update," *New York Times*, August 5, 2011.

3 John Hedley Brooke, *Science and Religion: Some Historical Perspectives* (New York: Cambridge University Press, 1991), 192–225; Peter Harrison, *The Territories of Science and Religion* (Chicago: University of Chicago Press, 2015), 148–153.

4 Harrison, *Territories of Science and Religion*, 148–153; John C. Burnham, *How Superstition Won and Science Lost: Popularization of Science and Health in the United States* (New Brunswick: Rutgers University Press, 1987), 144–146.

5 Louis Agassiz, "The Study of Nature," *Pennsylvania School Journal* (1862): 317; Harrison, *Territories of Science and Religion*, 148–153.

6 J. V. Jensen, "Thomas Henry Huxley's Lecture Tour of the United States, 1876," *Notes and Records of the Royal Society of London* 42, no. 2 (1988): 189.

7 Burnham, *How Superstition Won and Science Lost*, 127–169. E. L. Youmans, ed. *The Culture Demanded by Modern Life* (New York: D. Appleton and Company, 1867).

8 David Meshoulam, "Models of Science: Biographies in Early Twentieth-Century American High-School Science Textbooks" (master's thesis, University of Wisconsin–Madison, 2007); G. Stanley Hall, *Adolescence: Its Psychology and Its Relations to Physiology, Anthropology, Sociology, Sex, Crime, Religion, and Education*, vol. II (New York: D. Appleton, 1904), 150, 155.

9 John F. Woodhull, "Science for Culture," *School Review* 15 (1907): 129; see also Josiah P. Cooke, *Scientific Culture* (London: Henry S. King & Co., 1876).

10 S. Ralph Powers, "What Are Some of the Contributions of Science to Liberal Education?" in *The Thirty-First Yearbook of the National Society for the Study of Education (NSSE): A Program for Teaching Science* (Chicago: University of Chicago Press, 1932), 28, 34.

11 Stephen P. Weldon, *The Scientific Spirit of American Humanism* (Baltimore: Johns Hopkins University Press, 2020).

12 James B. Conant, *On Understanding Science: An Historical Approach* (New Haven: Yale University Press, 1947), 1.

13 Committee on General Education in a Free Society, *General Education in a Free Society: Report of the Harvard Committee* (Cambridge, MA: Harvard University Press, 1945), 155.

14 Conant, *On Understanding Science*, 19, 1. For details of Conant's general-science work, see Christopher Hamlin, "The Pedagogical Roots of the History of Science: Revisiting the Vision of James Bryant Conant," *Isis* 107 (2016): 282–308.

15 Audra J. Wolfe, *Competing with the Soviets: Science, Technology, and the State in Cold War America* (Baltimore: Johns Hopkins University Press, 2013); Richard Hofstadter, *Anti-Intellectualism in American Life* (New York: Vintage Books, 1962); W. Patrick McCray, "Snow's Storm," *Science* 364 (2019): 430–432. See also, Jewett, *Science under Fire*, 126.

16 I. I. Rabi, "Scientist and Humanist: Can the Minds Meet?" *Atlantic Monthly* (January 1956): 64, 67.

17 J. A. Stratton, "Science and the Educated Man," *Physics Today* (April 1956): 18, 20.

18 Gerald Holton, *Introduction to Concepts and Theories in Physical Science* (Cambridge, MA: Addison Wesley, 1952), xiii, xv. See also David

Meshoulam, "'Teaching Physics as One of the Humanities': The History of (Harvard) Project Physics, 1961-1970" (PhD diss., University of Wisconsin-Madison, 2014), 31–36.

19 Gerald Holton and Stephen G. Brush, *Physics, the Human Adventure: From Copernicus to Einstein and Beyond* (New Brunswick: Rutgers University Press, 2001), 1.

20 Gerald Holton, "On the Educational Philosophy of the Project Physics Course," in *The Scientific Imagination: Case Studies* (New York: Cambridge University Press, 1978), 294–295. See also Gerald Holton, "Physics and Culture," *Physics Bulletin* 14 (1963): 321–329.

21 AAAS, *Science for All Americans*, 21.

22 AAAS, *Science for All Americans*, 47, 111, 29, 133.

23 Project 2061 National Council Meeting, meeting transcript, November 12–13, 1987, Project 2061 Papers, AAAS Archives, Washington, DC.

24 Committee of the Corporation and the Academical Faculty, *Reports on the Course of Instruction in Yale College* (New Haven, CN, 1828), 7.

25 William P. Atkinson, *The Liberal Education of the Nineteenth Century* (New York: D. Appleton and Company, 1873), 4–5.

26 Caroline Winterer, *The Culture of Classicism: Ancient Greece and Rome in American Intellectual Life, 1780–1910* (Baltimore: Johns Hopkins University Press, 2002); Youmans, *Culture Demanded by Modern Life*, 1–56.

27 Albert L. Arey, "The Educational Value of the Physical Sciences," in Franklin W. Barrows, "The New York State Science Teachers Association," *Science* 5 (1897): 461–463 [emphasis in original]; Charles W. Eliot, "The Laboratory Method of Teaching," *School Journal* 72 (1906): 212.

28 Stephen A. Forbes, "Natural History in the Public Schools," *Illinois Schoolmaster* 6 (1873): 369; William North Rice, "Science Teaching in the Schools," *American Naturalist* 22 (1888): 770. See also John L. Rudolph, "The Lost Moral Purpose of Science Education," *Science Education* 104 (2020): 895–906; and David Hollinger, "Inquiry and Uplift: Late Nineteenth-Century American Academics and the Moral Efficacy of Scientific Practice," in *The Authority of Experts: Studies in History and Theory*, ed. Thomas L. Haskell (Bloomington: Indiana University Press, 1984), 142–156.

29 Rudolph, *How We Teach Science*, 58–96.

30 John Dewey to Scudder Klyce, April 23, 1915 (document 03517), Correspondence of John Dewey, electronic resource, ed. Barbara Levine, Anne Sharpe, and Harriet Furst Simon, Center for Dewey Studies,

Southern Illinois University at Carbondale; John Dewey, *How We Think* (Boston: D. C. Heath, 1910), 72.

31 George W. Hunter, *A Civic Biology, Presented in Problems* (New York: American Book Company, 1914), 7. Textbooks that included practical applications and the problem approach include Charles E. Dull, *Essentials of Modern Physics* (New York: Henry Holt, 1922); Henry S. Carhart and Horatio N. Chute, *Practical Physics*, rev. ed. (Boston: Allyn and Bacon, 1927); and William McPherson and William Edwards Henderson, *Chemistry and Its Uses: A Textbook for Secondary Schools* (New York: Ginn, 1922).

32 John L. Rudolph, "Turning Science to Account: Chicago and the General Science Movement in Secondary Education, 1905-1920," *Isis* 96 (2005): 353–389.

33 Committee on Teaching Science, *NSSE Thirty-First Yearbook: A Program for Teaching Science*, 40; Committee on Teaching Science, *NSSE Forty-Sixth Yearbook: Science Education in American Schools* (Chicago: University of Chicago Press, 1947), 145. On the close identification of problem solving, scientific method, and Dewey, see George W. Hunter, *Science Teaching at Junior and Senior High School Levels* (New York: American Book Company, 1934), 213; and Elwood D. Heiss, Ellsworth S. Obourn, and Charles W. Hoffman, *Modern Science Teaching* (New York: Macmillan Company, 1950), 48–49. On Dewey's scientific method, see Henry M. Cowles, *The Scientific Method: An Evolution of Thinking from Darwin to Dewey* (Cambridge, MA: Harvard University Press, 2020).

34 National Committee on Science Teaching, *Science Teaching for Better Living: A Philosophy or Point of View* (Washington, DC: American Council of Science Teachers, 1942), 32, 34, 10.

35 Paul L. Dressel, "How the Individual Learns Science," in *NSSE Fifty-Ninth Yearbook: Rethinking Science Education* (Chicago: University of Chicago Press, 1960), 45–46, 34. On the rise of cognitive psychology during this period, see Jamie Cohen-Cole, *The Open Mind: Cold War Politics and the Sciences of Human Nature* (Chicago: University of Chicago Press, 2014).

36 Educational Policies Commission, *Education and the Spirit of Science* (Washington, DC: National Education Association, 1966), 1.

37 Educational Policies Commission, *Education and the Spirit of Science*, 15, 16.

38 National Research Council, *Exploring the Intersection of Science Education and 21st Century Skills: A Workshop Summary* (Washington, DC: National Academies Press, 2010).

39 Stephen A. Forbes, "History and Status of Public School Science Work in Illinois," in *Educational Papers by Illinois Science Teachers, 1889-1890* (Peoria: J. W. Franks and Sons, 1891), 8, 14; see also Louis I. Kuslan, "Science in the 19th Century Normal School," *Science Education* 40 (1956): 138–144.

40 Herbert M. Kliebard, *The Struggle for the American Curriculum, 1893-1958*, 3rd ed. (New York: Routledge, 2004), 105–129.

41 Commission on the Reorganization of Secondary Education, *Reorganization of Science in Secondary Schools*, Bureau of Education Bulletin No. 26 (Washington, DC: Government Printing Office, 1920), 12–14.

42 Otis W. Caldwell and Edwin E. Slosson, eds., *Science Remaking the World* (New York: Garden City Publishing Company, 1927), vi, vii.

43 Edgar F. Van Buskirk and Edith Lillian Smith, *The Science of Everyday Life* (Boston: Houghton Mifflin, 1930); Henry S. Carhart and Horatio N. Chute, *Practical Physics* (Boston: Allyn and Bacon, 1920); William McPherson, William Edwards Henderson, and George Winegar Fowler, *Chemistry at Work* (Boston: Ginn and Company, 1938); and John W. Ritchie, *Biology and Human Affairs* (New York: World Book Company, 1941).

44 M. H. Trytten, "Scientists," *Scientific American* 185 (September 1951), 71; Arthur S. Flemming, "Mobilization," *Scientific American* 185 (September 1951), 93.

45 Quotations from Rudolph, *Scientists in the Classroom*, 62, 75.

46 "Red Scientists Start Early," *Business Week*, November 16, 1957, 126; "Crisis in Education," *Life*, March 24, 1958 and March 31, 1958.

47 Wayne J. Urban, *More than Science and Sputnik: The National Defense Education Act of 1958* (Tuscaloosa: University of Alabama Press, 2010); and Rudolph, *Scientists in the Classroom*.

48 David Kaiser, "Cold War Requisitions, Scientific Manpower, and the Production of American Physicists after World War II," *Historical Studies in the Physical and Biological Sciences* 33 (2002): 131–159; Daniel J. Kevles, *The Physicists: The History of a Scientific Community in Modern America*, 2nd ed. (Cambridge, MA: Harvard University Press, 1995), 410–426.

49 Roger L. Geiger, *The History of American Higher Education: Learning and Culture from the Founding to World War II* (Princeton: Princeton University Press, 2015), 281–287.

50 Newton Bateman, "Laying of Corner Stone of New University Building, and Dedication of New Mechanical Shops," in *Fourth Annual Report of the Board of Trustees of the Illinois Industrial University for the Year 1870–1* (Springfield: Illinois Journal Printing Office, 1872), 359.

51 National Science Foundation, *Science and Engineering Education for the 1980s and Beyond* (Washington, DC: National Science Foundation, 1980), xxiii; see also Productivity Improvement Research Section, *The Process of Technological Innovation: Reviewing the Literature* (Washington, DC: National Science Foundation, 1983); Elizabeth Popp Berman, *Creating the Market University: How Academic Science Became an Economic Engine* (Princeton: Princeton University Press, 2012), 40–57; and James T. Patterson, *Restless Giant: The United States from Watergate to* Bush v. Gore (New York: Oxford University Press, 2005), 7, 62–65.

52 D. J. R. Bruckner, "Science Has Its Back to the Wall," *Los Angeles Times*, April 13, 1970, A6.

53 National Commission on Excellence in Education, *A Nation at Risk: The Imperative for Educational Reform* (Washington, DC: US Government Printing Office, 1983), 7, 8; Jal Mehta, *The Allure of Order: High Hopes, Dashed Expectations, and the Troubled Quest to Remake American Schooling* (New York: Oxford University Press, 2013), 84–117.

54 National Science Board Commission on Precollege Education in Mathematics, Science and Technology, *Educating Americans for the 21st Century* (Washington, DC: National Science Foundation, 1983).

55 National Academies Committee on Prospering in the Global Economy of the 21st Century, *Rising above the Gathering Storm: Energizing and Employing America for a Brighter Economic Future* (Washington, DC: National Academies Press, 2005), 1, 3.

56 Rudolph, *How We Teach Science*, 217–221.

57 Carnegie Corporation of New York and Institute for Advanced Study, *The Opportunity Equation: Transforming Mathematics and Science Education for the Global Economy* (New York: Carnegie Corporation, 2009), vii.

58 National Research Council, *Framework for K-12 Science Education*; NGSS website: https://www.nextgenscience.org.

59 Forbes, "History and Status of Public School Science Work in Illinois," 14.

60 Morris Meister, "Science in Elementary and Secondary Education," *Science Education* 15 (1948): 13, 15; Carnegie Corporation of New York and Institute for Advanced Study, *The Opportunity Equation*, vii.

61 For a fascinating look at how the science education-for-citizenship argument shifted during the twentieth century, see Sevan G. Terzian, *Science Education and Citizenship: Fairs, Clubs, and Talent Searches for American Youth, 1918–1958* (New York: Palgrave Macmillan, 2013) .

62 Thomas D. Snyder, *120 Years of American Education: A Statistical Portrait* (Washington, DC: US Department of Education, Office of Educational Research and Improvement, National Center for Education Statistics, 1993); Edward A. Krug, *The Shaping of the American High School, 1880-1920* (Madison: University of Wisconsin Press, 1969), 6–7; William J. Reese, *The Origins of the American High School* (New Haven: Yale University Press, 1995), 260.

63 Commission on the Reorganization of Secondary Education, *Cardinal Principles of Secondary Education* (Washington, DC: Government Printing Office, 1918), 8, 9.

64 Commission on the Reorganization of Secondary Education, *Reorganization of Science in Secondary Schools*, 16, 11.

65 Committee on Teaching Science, *NSSE Thirty-First Yearbook: A Program for Teaching Science*, 42–43.

66 Edward A. Purcell, Jr., *The Crisis of Democratic Theory: Scientific Naturalism and the Problem of Value* (Lexington: University Press of Kentucky, 1973), 117–158; Jewett, *Science under Fire*, 8–20.

67 David A. Hollinger, "The Defense of Democracy and Robert K. Merton's Formulation of the Scientific Ethos," *Knowledge and Society: Studies in the Sociology of Culture Past and Present* 4 (1983): 1–15.

68 Reuben T. Shaw, "Toward More Exact Knowledge," *Science Education* 23 (1939): 359; John Dewey, *Freedom and Culture* (New York: G. P. Putman's Sons, 1939).

69 National Committee on Science Teaching, *Science Teaching for Better Living*, 34, 37.

70 Committee on General Education in a Free Society, *General Education in a Free Society*, 54; Cohen-Cole, *The Open Mind*, 13–34.

71 President's Science Advisory Committee (PSAC), *Education for the Age of Science* (Washington, DC: US Government Printing Office, 1959), 3.

72 PSAC, *Education for the Age of Science*, 6, 5.

73 Bentley Glass, "Liberal Education in a Scientific Age," *Bulletin of the Atomic Scientists* 14 (1958): 349.

74 James Trefil, *Why Science?* (New York: Teachers College Press, 2008), 34, 35.

75 National Research Council, *Taking Science to School: Learning and Teaching Science in Grades K-8* (Washington DC: National Academies Press, 2007), 2, 34.

76 John Hardwig, "Epistemic Dependence," *Journal of Philosophy* 82 (1985): 335–349; Harry Collins, "Rejecting Knowledge Claims Inside and Outside Science," *Social Studies of Science* 44 (2014): 722–735.

77 National Research Council, *National Science Education Standards*, 13.

Chapter 2

1 On school evaluation schemes, see Jack Schneider, *Beyond Test Scores: A Better Way to Measure School Quality* (Cambridge, MA: Harvard University Press, 2017).

2 Information on Project Lead the Way is at https://www.pltw.org.

3 Jack Schneider, *Excellence for All: How a New Breed of Reformers Is Transforming America's Public Schools* (Nashville: Vanderbilt University Press, 2011), 105–134; Robert H. Tai, "Posing Tougher Questions about the Advanced Placement Program," *Liberal Education* 94 (2008); 38–43; Rudolph, *How We Teach Science*, 220.

4 John Tierney, "AP Classes Are a Scam," *Atlantic Monthly* (October 2012) Christopher Drew, "Rethinking Advanced Placement," *New York Times*, January 7, 2011; Eugene Judson, "How Science and Math Teachers Address Different Course Levels: Advanced Placement (AP), Honors, and Regular," *High School Journal* 100 (2017): 226–249; William B. Wood, "Revising the AP Biology Curriculum," *Science* 325 (2009): 1627–1628; Serena Magrogan, "Past, Present, and Future of AP Chemistry: A Brief History of Course and Exam Alignment Efforts," *Journal of Chemical Education* 91 (2014): 1357–1361.

5 National Research Council, *America's Lab Report: Investigations in High School Science* (Washington, DC: National Academies Press, 2006), 6, 9.

6 Jal Mehta and Sarah Fine, *In Search of Deeper Learning: The Quest to Remake the American High School* (Cambridge, MA: Harvard University Press, 2019), 6.

Chapter 3

1 Letter of Business Community Support for NGSS. Retrieved June 17, 2021 from https://www.nextgenscience.org/sites/default/files/NGSS%20Business%20Support%20Letter%20REVISED%206.25.14.pdf.

2 Institute of Education Sciences, *Digest of Education Statistics 2020*, National Center for Education Statistics (Washington, DC: US Department of Education, 2021), table 201.20.

3 Institute of Education Sciences, *Report on the Condition of Education 2021* (Washington, DC: US Department of Education, 2021), chapter 2, High School Persistence and Completion. Retrieved June 17, 2021 from https://nces.ed.gov/programs/coe/indicator_coi.asp.

4 Institute of Education Sciences, *Digest of Education Statistics 2020*, table 104.20.

5 Kurt J. Bauman and Nikki L. Graf, *Educational Attainment: 2000, Census 2000 Brief* (Washington, DC: US Department of Commerce, 2003).

6 Institute of Education Sciences, *Digest of Education Statistics 2019*, table 318.20.

7 Liana Christin Landivar, *The Relationship between Science and Engineering Education and Employment in STEM Occupations*, report number ACS-23 (Washington, DC: US Department of Commerce, 2013).

8 The study defines the STEM occupations as the usual jobs you would expect, including computer occupations (programmers, computer systems analysts, web developers, and so on), engineering, biological scientist, astronomers, chemical technicians, etc. The STEM-related occupations include occupations such as architects, dieticians, podiatrists, recreational therapists, nurses, midwives, paramedics, medical records technicians, etc.

9 Paul Doty and Dorothy Zinberg, "Undergraduate Science Education: An Overview," *American Scientist* 60 (1972): 692. The corresponding percentage of non-engineering, natural science graduates in 2017 was just over 4%, a significant increase certainly from 2%, but overall still only a small fraction of all high school graduates.

10 The NSF education funding levels graphed include all programs within that category, including graduate fellowships alongside K–12 research and curriculum funding. The funding data are a sample of convenience meant to generally reflect the foundation's commitment to science education at all levels over these years.

11 Landivar, *Relationship between Science and Engineering Education and Employment in STEM Occupations.*

12 Jonathan Rothwell, *The Hidden STEM Economy* (Washington, DC: Brookings Institution, 2013).

13 Robert Bozick, Sinduja Srinivasan, and Michael Gottfried, "Do High School STEM Courses Prepare Non-College Bound Youth for Jobs in the STEM Economy," *Education Economics* 25 (2017): 246. This study confirmed other studies that similarly found no significant connection between high school science course taking and increased earnings after high school; see Joseph G. Altonji, "The Effects of High School Curriculum on Education and Labor Market Outcomes," *Journal of Human Resources* 30 (1995): 409–438; Phillip Levine and David Zimmerman, "The Benefit of Additional High-School Math and Science Classes for Young Men and Women," *Journal of Business and Economic Statistics* 13 (1995): 137–149; and Heather Rose and Julian R. Betts, "The Effect of High School Courses on Earnings," *Review of Economics and Statistics* 86 (2004): 497–513.

14 Rothwell, *The Hidden STEM Economy*, 10.

15 https://www.bls.gov/emp/tables/stem-employment.htm; https://www.bls.gov/emp/tables/occupational-projections-and-characteristics.htm.

16 Hal Salzman and Beryl Leif Benderly, "STEM Performance and Supply: Assessing the Evidence for Education Policy," *Journal of Science Education and Technology* 28 (2019): 23; Yu Xie and Alexandra A. Killewald, *Is American Science in Decline?* (Cambridge, MA: Harvard University Press, 2012); Michael S. Teitelbaum, *Falling Behind? Boom, Bust, and the Global Race for Scientific Talent* (Princeton: Princeton University Press, 2014), 3.

17 Letter of Business Community Support for NGSS [emphasis added]. For a detailed analysis of the disciplinary/content focus of NGSS, see Andrew A. Zucker and Pendred Noyce, "A Response to the National Academies' 2021 Call to Action," *Science Educator* 28 (2022): 55–62.

18 Camera, "U.S. Students Show No Improvement in Math, Reading, Science on International Exam."

19 Andreas Schleicher, *PISA 2018: Insights and Interpretations* (Paris: OECD Publishing, 2019); Institute for Education Sciences, *TIMSS 2019 U.S. Highlights Web Report,* NCES 2021-021 (Washington, DC: US Department of Education, 2021).

20 Next Generation Science Standards, *The Need for Standards*. Retrieved June 18, 2021 from https://www.nextgenscience.org/need-standards #Lagging.

21 Eric A. Hanushek and Ludger Woessmann, "Measurement Counts: International Student Tests and Economic Growth," *International-Education Blog*, October 1, 2019. Retrieved June 18, 2021 from http://hanushek.stanford.edu/publications/measurement-counts-international-student-tests-and-economic-growth.

22 Francisco O. Ramirez, Xiaowei Luo, Evan Schofer, and John W. Meyer, "Student Achievement and National Economic Growth," *American Journal of Education* 113 (2006): 23.

23 Jeremy Rappleye and Hikaru Komatsu, "Is Knowledge Capital Theory Degenerate? PIAAC, PISA, and Economic Growth," *Compare* 51 (2021): 253. Other critiques of the test-score/economic-growth link include Gili S. Drori, "Science Education and Economic Development: Trends, Relationships, and Research Agenda," *Studies in Science Education* 35 (2000): 27–57; David H. Kamens, "A Maturing Global Testing Regime Meets the World Economy: Test Scores and Economic Growth, 1960-2012," *Comparative Education Review* 59 (2015): 420–446; Nelly P. Stromquist, "Using Regression Analysis to Predict Countries' Economic Growth: Illusion and Fact in Education Policy," *Real-World Economics Review* 76 (2016): 65–74; and Hikaru Komatsu and Jeremy Rappleye, "A New Global Policy Regime Founded on Invalid Statistics? Hanushek, Woessmann, PISA, and Economic Growth," *Comparative Education* 53 (2017): 166–191.

24 Desilver, "U.S. Students' Academic Achievement Still Lags that of Their Peers in Many Other Countries"; "World Economic Outlook Database, April 2021," *World Economic Outlook* (International Monetary Fund, April 2021).

25 Mark Boroush, U.S. R&D Increased by $32 Billion in 2017, to $548 Billion; Estimate for 2018 Indicates a Further Rise to $580 Billion, NSF 20-309 (Washington, DC: National Center for Science and Engineering Statistics/National Science Foundation, January 2020) .

Chapter 4

1 Herbert G. Espy, *The Public Secondary School: A Critical Analysis of Secondary Education in the United States* (Boston: Houghton Mifflin, 1939), 239.

2 Fred. D. Barber, "The Present Status and Real Meaning of General Science," *School Science and Mathematics* 15 (1915): 218–219.

3 George S. Counts, *The Senior High School Curriculum* (Chicago: University of Chicago Press, 1926), 75.

4 Rudolph, "Turning Science to Account," 353–389.

5 G. P. H. [Gaylord P. Harnwell], "A New Foundation," *Review of Scientific Instruments* 16 (1945): 269. See also Dwight E. Sollberger, "A Message from the Elementary Science Editor: Two Hundred Years Late," *The Science Teacher* 14, no. 1 (1947): 30; Morris Meister, "Science in Elementary and Secondary Education," *The Science Teacher* 15, no. 1 (1948): 13; and Bess Furman, "Atomic Age Needs in School Assayed," *New York Times*, December 29, 1948.

6 Robert H. Carleton, "Science Teaching and Education Aims Today," *Phi Delta Kappan* 33 (1951): 104.

7 Carleton, "Science Teaching and Education Aims Today," 101.

8 William D. McElroy, "The Role of Fundamental Research in an Advanced Society," *American Scientist* 59 (1971): 295, 297; John H. Douglas, "A Double-Barreled Challenge for Science Education," *Science News* 105 (1974): 136–138.

9 Milton O. Pella, George T. O'Hearn, and Calvin W. Gale, "Referents to Scientific Literacy," *Journal of Research in Science Teaching* 4 (1966): 199–208; Benjamin S. P. Shen, "Science Literacy," *American Scientist* 63 (1975): 265–268; *Daedalus* 112 (1983).

10 Philip M. Boffey, "In Age of Technology, the Three R's Are Not Enough," *New York Times*, May 16, 1982, E8. See also National Science Foundation, *Science & Engineering Education for the 1980's & Beyond* (Washington, DC: US Government Printing Office, 1980).

11 J. Stanley Ahmann, Robert Crane, Donald Searls, and Robert Larson, "Science Achievement: The Trend Is Down," *The Science Teacher* 42, no. 7 (1975): 23–25; Gene I. Maeroff, "School Science Struggles Less Successfully Than Ever," *New York Times*, July 2, 1978, p. E16.

12 Quotation from William Hively, "How Much Science Does the Public Understand?" *American Scientist* 76 (1988): 441; Connie Lauerman, "Failing Science," *Chicago Tribune*, August 7, 1988, p. J8; Jon D. Miller, "The Measurement of Civic Scientific Literacy," *Public Understanding of Science* 7 (1998): 203–223.

13 National Science Board, *Science and Engineering Indicators 1989* (Washington, DC: US Government Printing Office, 1989); National

Science Board, *Science and Engineering Indicators 2006* (Arlington, VA: National Science Foundation, 2006), 7–17; Robert M. Hazen and James Trefil, *Science Matters: Achieving Scientific Literacy* (New York: Doubleday, 1991), xii. For the most recent version of the science and engineering indicators, see https://ncses.nsf.gov/indicators.

14 National Academies of Sciences, Engineering, and Medicine, *Science Literacy: Concepts, Contexts, and Consequences* (Washington, DC: National Academies Press, 2016).

Chapter 5

1 James Trefil, "Scientific Literacy," *Annals of the New York Academy of Sciences* 775 (1995): 548–549.

2 Forbes, "History and Status of Public School Science Work in Illinois," 14.

3 Andrew Pawl, Analia Barrantes, David E. Pritchard, and Rudolph Mitchell, "What Do Seniors Remember from Freshman Physics?" *Physical Review Special Topics–Physics Education Research* 8 (2012): 020118; Stephen D. Schneid, Hal Pashler, and Chris Armour, "How Much Basic Science Content Do Second-Year Medical Students Remember from Their First Year?" *Medical Teacher* 41 (2019): 231–233; and Amber Todd and William Romine, "The Learning Loss Effect in Genetics: What Ideas Do Students Retain or Lose after Instruction?" *CBE–Life Sciences Education* 17 (2018): 1–17.

4 National Science Board, "Public Familiarity with S&T Facts," in *Science and Engineering Indicators 2020*.

5 Tobias Gerstenberg and Joshua B. Tenenbaum, "Intuitive Theories," in *Oxford Handbook of Causal Reasoning*, ed. Michael Waldmann (New York: Oxford University Press, 2017), 515–548.

6 Andrew Shtulman, *Scienceblind: Why Our Intuitive Theories about the World Are So Often Wrong* (New York: Basic Books, 2017).

7 Gerstenberg and Tenenbaum, "Intuitive Theories," 515.

8 Rainer Bromme and Susan R. Goldman, "The Public's Bounded Understanding of Science," *Educational Psychologist* 49 (2014): 59–69; Noah Weeth Feinstein and David Isaac Waddington, "Individual Truth Judgments or Purposeful Collective Sensemaking? Rethinking Science Education's Response to the Post-Truth Era," *Educational Psychologist* 55 (2020): 155–166; Brian G. Southwell, *Social Networks and*

Popular Understanding of Science and Health: Sharing Disparities (Baltimore: Johns Hopkins University Press, 2013); Jim Ryder, "Identifying Science Understanding for Functional Scientific Literacy," *Studies in Science Education* 36 (2001): 1–44.

9 Alan Irwin and Brian Wynne, eds., *Misunderstanding Science? The Public Reconstruction of Science and Technology* (New York: Cambridge University Press, 1996) ; Brian Wynne, "Misunderstood misunderstanding: Social Identities and Public Uptake of Science," *Public Understanding of Science* 1 (1992): 281–304.

10 John L. Rudolph and Shusaku Horibe, "What Do We Mean by Science Education for Civic Engagement?" *Journal of Research in Science Teaching* 53 (2016): 805–820.

11 Matthew C. Nisbet and Dietram A. Sheufele, "What's Next for Science Communication? Promising Directions and Lingering Distractions," *American Journal of Botany* 96 (2009): 1767. On socioscientific issues, see, for example, Troy D. Sadler and Samantha R. Fowler, "A Threshold Model of Content Knowledge Transfer for Socioscientific Argumentation," *Science Education* 90 (2006): 986–1004; Karin Rudsberg and Johan Öhman, "The Role of Knowledge in Participatory and Pluralistic Approaches to ESE," *Environmental Education Research* 21 (2015): 955–974; Marcus M. Grace and Mary Ratcliffe, "The Science and Values that Young People Draw Upon to Make Decisions about Biological Conservation Issues," *International Journal of Science Education* 24 (2002): 1157–1169; Troy D. Sadler, "Informal Reasoning Regarding Socioscientific Issues: A Critical Review of the Research," *Journal of Research in Science Teaching* 41 (2004): 513–536; Virginie Albe, "Students' Positions and Considerations of Scientific Evidence About a Controversial Socioscientific Issue," *Science & Education* 17 (2008): 805–827; William A. Sandoval, Beate Sodian, Susanne Koerber, and Jacqueline Wong, "Developing Children's Early Competencies to Engage with Science," *Educational Psychologist* 49 (2014): 139–152; and Sihan Xiao and William A. Sandoval, "Associations Between Attitudes Towards Science and Children's Evaluation of Information About Socioscientific Issues," *Science & Education* 26 (2017): 247–269.

12 Gale M. Sinatra and Barbara K. Hofer, *Science Denial: Why It Happens and What to Do about It* (New York: Oxford University Press, 2021); Patrick W. Kraft, Milton Lodge, and Charles S. Taber, "Why People 'Don't Trust the Evidence': Motivated Reasoning and Scientific Beliefs,"

Annals of the American Academy of Political and Social Science 658 (2019): 121–133; Jan Alexis Nielsen, "Science in Discussions: An Analysis of the Use of Science Content in Socioscientific Discussions," *Science Education* 96 (2012): 428–456; Gale M. Sinatra, Dorothe Kienhues, and Barbara K. Hofer, "Addressing Challenges to Public Understanding of Science: Epistemic Cognition, Motivated Reasoning, and Conceptual Change," *Educational Psychologist* 49 (2014): 123–138.

13 Dan M. Kahan, Ellen Peters, Maggie Wittlin, Paul Slovic, Lisa Larrimore Ouelette, Donald Braman, and Gregory Mandel, "The Polarizing Impact of Science Literacy and Numeracy on Perceived Climate Change Risks," *Nature Climate Change* 2 (2012): 734.

14 F. James Rutherford, Gerald Holton, and Fletcher G. Watson, *Project Physics* (New York: Holt, Rinehart and Winston, 1981), 36–59, 485–490.

15 "Topic Arrangements of the Next Generation Science Standards," Achieve Inc., 2013. https://www.nextgenscience.org/sites/default/files/AllTopic.pdf

16 A Private Universe, directed by Matthew H. Schneps and Philip Sadler (Harvard-Smithsonian Center for Astrophysics, 1987).

17 Sandra Feder, "Physicist and Educator Says New Pedagogy Imperative for Society," Stanford School of Humanities and Science, December 8, 2020 https://humsci.stanford.edu/feature/physicist-and-educator-says-new-pedagogy-imperative-society.

Chapter 6

1 Project 2061 National Council Meeting, meeting transcript, November 12–13, 1987, Project 2061 Papers.

2 Rudolph, *How We Teach Science*, 159–179; Stanley L. Helgeson, Patricia E. Blosser, and Robert W. Howe, *The Status of Pre-College Science, Mathematics, and Social Science Education: 1955–1975*, vol. 1, Science Education (Washington, DC: National Science Foundation, 1977); and Robert E. Stake and Jack A. Easley Jr., *Case Studies in Science Education*, vol. II, *Design, Overview and General Findings* (Washington, DC: National Science Foundation, 1978).

3 Daniel K. Capps and Barbara A. Crawford, "Inquiry-Based Instruction and Teaching about Nature of Science: Are They Happening?" *Journal of Science Teacher Education* 24 (2013): 520; National Research Council, *America's Lab Report*; Mehta and Fine, *In Search of Deeper Learning*. For

a detailed history of this failure, see Rudolph, *How We Teach Science*, 211–217.

4 Mark Windschitl, "Folk Theories of 'Inquiry:' How Preservice Teachers Reproduce the Discourse and Practices of an Atheoretical Scientific Method," *Journal of Research in Science Teaching* 41 (2004): 481–512; Margaret R. Blanchard, Sherry A. Southerland, and Ellen M. Granger, "No Silver Bullet for Inquiry: Making Sense of Teacher Change Following an Inquiry-Based Research Experience for Teachers," *Science Education* 93 (2009): 322–360; Daniel K. Capps, Jonathan T. Shemwell, and Ashley M. Young, "Over Reported and Misunderstood? A Study of Teachers' Reported Enactment and Knowledge of Inquiry-Based Science Teaching," *International Journal of Science Education* 38 (2016): 934–959.

5 Clark A. Chinn and Betina A. Malhotra, "Epistemologically Authentic Inquiry in Schools: A Theoretical Framework for Evaluating Inquiry Tasks," *Science Education* 86 (2002): 175.

6 Troy D. Sadler and Lyle McKinney, "Scientific Research for Undergraduate Students: A Review of the Literature," *Journal of College Science Teaching* 39 (2010): 43–49.

7 Troy D. Sadler, Stephen Burgin, Lyle McKinney, and Luis Ponjuan, "Learning Science through Research Apprenticeships: A Critical Review of the Literature," *Journal of Research in Science Teaching* 47 (2010): 251; Randy L. Bell, Lesley M. Blair, Barbara A. Crawford, and Norman G. Lederman, "Just Do It? Impact of a Science Apprenticeship Program on High School Students' Understandings of the Nature of Science and Scientific Inquiry," *Journal of Research in Science Teaching* 40 (2003): 487–509; William A. Sandoval, "Understanding Students' Practical Epistemologies and Their Influence on Learning through Inquiry," *Science Education* 89 (2005): 634–656; and Marcia C. Linn, Erin Palmer, Anne Baranger, Elizabeth Gerard, and Elisa Stone, "Undergraduate Research Experiences: Impacts and Opportunities," *Science* 347 (2015): 627–633. On the history and limitations of citizen-science, see Bruno J. Strasser, Jérôme Baudry, Dana Mahr, Gabriela Sanchez, and Elise Tancoigne, "'Citizen Science'? Rethinking Science and Public Participation," *Science & Technology Studies* 32 (2019): 52–76; and Rick Bonney, Tina B. Phillips, Heidi L. Ballard, and Jody W. Enck, "Can Citizen Science Enhance Public Understanding of Science?" *Public Understanding of Science* 25 (2016): 2–16.

8   Committee on Strengthening Research Experiences for Undergraduate STEM Students, *Undergraduate Research Experiences for STEM Students: Successes, Challenges, and Opportunities* (Washington, DC: National Academies Press, 2017), 33–34.

9   David Klahr, Corinne Zimmerman, and Jamie Jirout, "Educational Interventions to Advance Children's Scientific Thinking," *Science* 333 (2011): 971–975; Corinne Zimmerman, "The Development of Scientific Reasoning Skills: What Psychologists Contribute to an Understanding of Elementary Science Learning," draft report to the National Research Council, Committee on Science Learning Kindergarten through Eighth Grade, August, 2005.

10 Andrew Shtulman and Caren Walker, "Developing an Understanding of Science," *Annual Review of Developmental Psychology* 2 (2020): 111–132; Petra Barchfeld and Beate Sodian, "Differentiating Theories from Evidence: The Development of Argument Evaluation Abilities in Adolescence and Early Adulthood," *Informal Logic* 29 (2009): 396–416; and National Academies of Sciences, Engineering, and Medicine, *Science and Engineering in Preschool through Elementary Grades: The Brilliance of Children and the Strengths of Educators* (Washington, DC: National Academies Press, 2021), 4–6, 4–8.

11 Lewis Wolpert, *The Unnatural Nature of Science* (Cambridge, MA: Harvard University Press, 1993); Beate Sodian and Merry Bullock, "Scientific Reasoning—Where Are We Now?" *Cognitive Development* 23 (2008): 432; and Bromme and Goldman, "The Public's Bounded Understanding of Science."

12 Shtulman and Walker, "Developing an Understanding of Science," 122; Sharon Bailin, "Critical Thinking and Science Education," *Science & Education* 11 (2002): 361–375.

13 Robin M. Hogarth, "Deciding Analytically or Trusting Your Intuition? The Advantages and Disadvantages of Analytic and Intuitive Thought," in Tilman Betsch and Susanne Haberstroh (eds.), *The Routines of Decision Making* (Hove Psychology, 2005), 67–82; Jonathan Baron, *Judgment Misguided: Intuition and Error in Public Decision Making* (New York: Oxford University Press, 1998); and Sadler, "Informal Reasoning Regarding Socioscientific Issues," 513–536.

14 Rudolph, *How We Teach Science.*

15 On the relationship of content teaching to scientific reasoning, see Lei Bao, Tianfan Cai, Kathy Koenig, Kai Fang, Jing Han, Jing Wang,

Qing Liu, Lin Ding, Lili Cui, Ying Luo, Yufeng Wang, Lieming Li, and Nianle Wu, "Learning and Scientific Reasoning," *Science* 323 (2009): 586–587.

Chapter 7

1 National Research Council, *Framework for K-12 Science Education*, 7.
2 Hardwig, "Epistemic Dependence," 335–349; Stephen P. Norris, "Learning to Live with Expertise: Toward a Theory of Intellectual Communalism for Guiding Science Teaching," *Science Education* 79 (1995): 201–217. See also Steven Shapin, "The Way We Trust Now: The Authority of Science and the Character of the Scientist," in *Trust Me, I'm a Scientist*, ed. P. Hoodbhoy, D. Glaser, and S. Shapin (London: British Council, 2004), 42–63; Friederike Hendriks, Dorothe Kienhues, and Rainer Bromme, "Trust in Science and the Science of Trust," in *Trust and Communication in a Digitized World*, ed. B. Blöbaum (New York: Springer, 2016), 143–159; and Tom Nichols, *The Death of Expertise: The Campaign against Established Knowledge and Why It Matters* (New York: Oxford University Press, 2018). On the need for rebuilding trust in biology education, see Adam Laats, *Creationism USA: Bridging the Impasse on Teaching Evolution* (New York: Oxford University Press, 2020).
3 James Bryant Conant, "Foreword," in *General Education in Science*, ed. I. B. Cohen and F. G. Watson (Cambridge, MA: Harvard University Press, 1952), xiii. Cohen and Watson, *General Education in Science*, vi–xi.
4 Kelly Moore, *Disrupting Science: Social Movements, American Scientists, and the Politics of the Military, 1945-1975* (Princeton: Princeton University Press, 2009); Kevles, *The Physicists*, 393–409.
5 Naomi Oreskes and Eric M. Conway, *Merchants of Doubt: How a Handful of Scientists Obscured the Truth on Issues from Tobacco Smoke to Global Warming* (New York: Bloomsbury Publishing, 2011) ; Edward J. Larson, *Trial and Error: The American Controversy Over Creation and Evolution*, 3rd edn. (New York: Oxford University Press, 2003); John H. Zammito, *A Nice Derangement of Epistemes: Postpositivism in the Study of Science from Quine to Latour* (Chicago: University of Chicago Press, 2004); Brad Plumer and Coral Davenport, "Science Under Attack: How Trump Is Sidelining Researchers and Their Work," *New York Times,* December 28, 2019; Adam Nagourney and Jeremy W. Peters, "Denial and Defiance: Trump

and His Base Downplay the Virus Ahead of the Election," *New York Times*, September 21, 2020.

6 The arrangement suggested here follows more or less that recommended by Harry Collins and Robert Evans in *Why Democracies Need Science* (Cambridge, UK: Polity Press, 2017).

7 For the most well-developed argument for a greater public role with respect to science, see Zeynep Pamuk, *Politics and Expertise: How to Use Science in a Democratic Society* (Princeton: Princeton University Press, 2021).

8 Brian Wynne, "Public Engagement as a Means of Restoring Public Trust in Science—Hitting the Notes, but Missing the Music?" *Community Genetics* 9 (2006): 211–220; Gordon Gauchat, "The Cultural Authority of Science: Public Trust and Acceptance of Organized Science," *Public Understanding of Science* 20 (2011): 751–770; National Science Board, "Public Attitudes about S&T in General," in *Science and Engineering Indicators 2020*.

9 Hamlin, "The Pedagogical Roots of the History of Science: Revisiting the Vision of James Bryant Conant," 282–308.

10 Deanna Kuhn and David Dean, Jr., "Is Developing Scientific Thinking All About Learning to Control Variables?" *Psychological Science* 16 (2005): 866–870; National Science Board, "Science and Technology: Public Attitudes, Knowledge, and Interest," in *Science and Engineering Indicators 2020*.

11 Adrian Currie, "Hot-Blooded Gluttons: Dependency, Coherence, and Method in the Historical Sciences," *British Journal for the Philosophy of Science* 68 (2017): 929–952. For an extended discussion of this point, see Charles R. Ault, Jr., *Challenging Science Standards: A Skeptical Critique of the Quest for Unity* (New York: Rowman and Littlefield, 2015).

12 Paul N. Edwards, *A Vast Machine: Computer Models, Climate Data, and the Politics of Global Warming* (Cambridge, MA: MIT Press, 2013); Naomi Oreskes, "The Scientific Consensus on Climate Change: How Do We Know We're Not Wrong?" in *Climate Change: What It Means for Us, Our Children, and Our Grandchildren*, 2nd edn., ed. J. F. C. DiMento and P. Doughman (Cambridge, MA: MIT Press, 2014), 66–99.

13 Nancy Cartwright, *The Dappled World* (Cambridge, UK: Cambridge University Press, 1999); Philip Kitcher, *Science, Truth, and Democracy* (New York: Oxford University Press, 2001); and Helen Longino, *The Fate of Knowledge* (Princeton: Princeton University Press, 2002). On

the mismatch between public views of science and actual practice, see John L. Rudolph and Jim Stewart, "Evolution and the Nature of Science: On the Historical Discord and Its Implications for Education," *Journal of Research in Science Teaching* 35 (1998): 1069–1089.

14 See, for example, Ryder, "Identifying Science Understanding for Functional Scientific Literacy," 1–44; Jim Ryder, "School Science Education for Citizenship: Strategies for Teaching About the Epistemology of Science," *Journal of Curriculum Studies* 34 (2002): 637–658; Richard A. Duschl, "Practical Reasoning and Decision Making in Science: Struggles for Truth," *Educational Psychologist* 55 (2020): 187–192; and, for an account of past efforts, Rudolph, *Scientists in the Classroom.*

15 Models for some of this can be found in Kitcher, *Science, Truth, and Democracy* and Pamuk, *Politics and Expertise.*

16 Oreskes and Conway, *Merchants of Doubt;* Larson, *Trial and Error;* Laats, *Creationism USA;* Andrew Zucker, "Teaching Scientific Literacy," *The Science Teacher* 88, no. 4 (2021): 8–9.

17 See, for example, Troy D. Sadler, "Situating Socio-scientific Issues in Classrooms as a Means of Achieving Goals of Science Education," in *Socio-scientific Issues in the Classroom,* ed. T. Sadler (Dordrecht: Springer, 2011), 1–9; and Noah Weeth Feinstein and Kathryn L. Kirchgasler, "Sustainability in Science Education? How the Next Generation Science Standards Approach Sustainability, and Why It Matters," *Science Education* 99 (2015): 121–144; and Andrew Zucker and Pendred Noyce, "Lessons from the Pandemic about Science Education," *Phi Delta Kappan* 102, no. 2 (2020): 44–49. Another worthwhile approach is described in Charles R. Ault, Jr., *Beyond Science Standards: Play, Art, Coherence, Community* (Lanham, MD: Rowman & Littlefield, 2021).

18 *Cosmos,* "The Shores of the Cosmic Ocean."

19 National Center for Science and Engineering Statistics, *Women, Minorities, and Persons with Disabilities in Science and Engineering: 2021* (Alexandria, VA: National Science Foundation, 2021); Elle Lett, H. Moses Murdock, Whitney U. Orji, Jaya Aysola, and Ronnie Sebro, "Trends in Racial/Ethnic Representation Among US Medical Students," *JAMA Network Open* 2 (2019): e1910490; American Association of Medical Colleges, *Diversity in Medicine: Facts and Figures 2019* (2019), https://www. aamc.org/data-reports/workforce/report/diversity-facts-figures; Pew Research Center, "STEM Jobs See Uneven Progress in Increasing Gender, Racial and Ethnic Diversity," April 2021.

20 Rebecca Skloot, *The Immortal Life of Henrietta Lacks* (New York: Crown Publishing, 2010); Vanessa Northington Gamble, "Under the Shadow of Tuskegee: African Americans and Health Care," *American Journal of Public Health* 87 (1997): 1773–1778; Londa Schiebinger, "Scientific Research Must Take Gender into Account," *Nature* 507 (2014): 9; Simar Singh Bajaj and Fatima Cody Stanford, "Beyond Tuskegee—Vaccine Distrust and Everyday Racism," *New England Journal of Medicine* 384 (2021): e12(1)–e12(2).

21 On trust and the social nature of science, see Longino, *The Fate of Knowledge*, and Naomi Oreskes, *Why Trust Science?* (Princeton: Princeton University Press, 2019).

22 Elaine Seymour and Nancy M. Hewitt, *Talking about Leaving* (Boulder, CO: Westview Press, 1997); Elaine Seymour and Anne-Barrie Hunter, eds., *Talking about Leaving Revisited: Persistence, Relocation, and Loss in Undergraduate STEM Education* (Springer, 2019).

23 Heidi B. Carlone and Angela Johnson, "Understanding the Science Experiences of Successful Women of Color: Science Identity as an Analytic Lens," *Journal of Research in Science Teaching* 44 (2007): 1187–1218; Jan E. Stets, Philip S. Brenner, Peter J. Burke, and Richard T. Serpe, "The Science Identity and Entering a Science Occupation," *Social Science Research* 64 (2017): 1–14; Ann Y. Kim and Gail M. Sinatra, "Science Identity Development: An Interactionist Approach," *International Journal of STEM Education* 5 (2018): 1–6; National Academy of Sciences, *Expanding Underrepresented Minority Participation: America's Science and Technology Talent at the Crossroads* (Washington, DC: National Academies Press, 2011); National Academies of Sciences, Engineering, and Medicine, *Promising Practices for Addressing the Underrepresentation of Women in Science, Engineering, and Medicine: Opening Doors* (Washington, DC: National Academies Press, 2020).

24 Many of the fundamental learning outcomes included here are well described by Oreskes in *Why Trust Science?*

Chapter 8

1 Rudolph, *How We Teach Science.*

2 I'm indebted to David Labaree for his work on the idea of credentialism in schooling; see his *Someone Has to Fail: The Zero-Sum Game of Public Schooling* (Cambridge, MA: Harvard University Press, 2010).

3 David F. Labaree, "Public Goods, Private Goods: The American Struggle Over Educational Goals," *American Educational Research Journal* 34 (1997): 39–81. The distinction between things with "use value" and "exchange value" was famously made in economics by Karl Marx in the nineteenth century.

4 William J. Reese, *America's Public Schools: From the Common School to "No Child Left Behind,"* updated edn. (Baltimore: Johns Hopkins University Press, 2011); Labaree, "Public Goods, Private Goods," 39–81.

5 Carol D. Lee, Gregory White, and Dian Dong, eds. *Educating for Civic Reasoning and Discourse* (Washington, DC: National Academy of Education, 2021), 1; Rebecca Winthrop, "The Need for Civic Education in 21st-Century Schools," *Brookings Institution,* https://www.brookings.edu/policy2020/bigideas/the-need-for-civic-education-in-21st-century-schools (2020).

6 Sandra K. Abell, "Research on Science Teacher Knowledge," in *Handbook of Research on Science Education,* ed. S. K. Abell, K. Appleton, and D. Hanuscin (New York: Routledge, 2007), 1105–1149.

7 National Science Board, "Elementary and Secondary Mathematics and Science Education," in *Science and Engineering Indicators 2016* (Alexandria, VA: National Science Foundation, 2016); Joanne K. Olson, Christine D. Tippett, Todd M. Milford, Chris Ohana, and Michael P. Clough, "Science Teacher Preparation in a North American Context," *Journal of Science Teacher Education* 26 (2015): 7–28.

8 See, for example, Julie Rowland Woods, *Mitigating Teacher Shortages: Alternative Teacher Certification* (Denver, CO: Education Commission of the States, 2016). For a discussion of the inadequacy of content-only preparation, see Charles J. Iaconangelo, Geoffrey Phelps, and Drew H. Gitomer, "Dimensionality and Validity of the Content Knowledge for Teaching Construct Using Cognitive Diagnostic Modeling and Known Groups Comparisons," *Teaching and Teacher Education* 114 (2022): 103690.

INDEX

Note: *f* denotes figure; *t* denotes table; SE is science education